HOSANNA! MUSIC®

Songbook 11

From the recordings:

We Draw Near, Shout To The Lord, God Can!, He Will Save You, Come To The Throne, Revival at Brownsville, Welcome Home

PRAISE worship®

Printing

8 9 10

FOREWORD

Praise and Worship Songbook Eleven includes all of the songs from the following Hosanna! Music albums:

Come to the Throne
God Can
He Will Save You
Revival at Brownsville
Shout to the Lord
We Draw Near
Welcome Home

Every song is arranged in four-part harmony (SATB) and can be easily performed by your choir or worship team. The four-part harmony also works well as a basis for piano and organ accompaniment. Cued notes have been added where necessary to help establish the "feel" of the song. Guitar chords are also provided.

Musicians should be encouraged to embellish these arrangements by improvising with the chord symbols. When there is a note under a slash (e.g., F/G), the note above the slash is the chord to be played by the upper register instruments (guitar, right hand of the piano, etc.). The note below the slash is to be played by the lower register instruments (bass guitar, organ pedals, left hand of the piano, etc.). For songs that flow smoothly with each other, a medley reference is listed on each appropriate page.

This songbook has many features to help you plan your worship services.

Index "A" lists all songs by key and tempo. Praise and worship times will flow more smoothly if you select songs that are closely related in key and tempo. Create medleys of songs rather than stopping after each song. Choose songs that are related thematically, such as:

Enemy's Camp	A Flat Major
Can You Believe	A Flat Major
We've Come to Praise Him	A Flat Major
Look What the Lord Has Done	A Flat Major

Index "B" lists the songs by topic, such as joy, thanksgiving, victory, etc. If you know the theme of your pastor's message, you can prepare the hearts of the people by focusing your worship on the same topic.

Index "C" lists songs by the first line of lyrics in case you are unsure of the title.

Index "D" lists the songs according to their Scriptural references. If you are searching for a song featuring a specific Scripture, you will find it listed in biblical order.

Index "E" lists copyright owners of the songs presented in this publication.

We wish to thank all those who have given their permission to print the songs in this book. Every effort has been made to locate the copyright owners. If any omissions have occurred, we will make proper corrections in future printings.

TABLE OF CONTENTS

You are worthy... to receive glory and honor and power... Revelation 4:11 (NIV)

886

All Glory and Honor

HM-69

Words and Music by
MARTIN J. NYSTROM,
GARY SADLER and DON HARRIS

Cm B♭2/D
2, 3.
E♭2/G
A♭2
As we're wait - ing here before You, with all
We are stand - ing in Your pres - ence, You have
E♭/B♭
A♭2/C
earth - ly nois - es stilled; Let the
made Your glo - ry known; We will
Fm7
E♭/G
sound of heav - en's wor - ship cause this
join the hosts of heav - en as they
F/A
G/B
tem - ple to be filled.
wor - ship at Your throne.
CHORUS
Cm Gm7 A♭2 E♭ B♭/D Cm
All glo - ry and hon - or, all

Gm7
Ab
Bb/Ab
Ab
Bb
pow - er and praise;
Cm
Gm7
Ab2
Eb
We join with the an - gels, giv-ing
2nd time to Coda
Fm
Cm7
Ebsus/Ab
Bbsus
Bb
glo - ry to Your name.
3. The
Coda
BRIDGE
Bbsus
Bb
Abmaj7
name. Like the roar of man - y wa -
Bb
Cm
Bb
ters, like a might-y rush - ing wind; Like the

A♭maj7
B♭sus
B♭
voic - es of thou - sands and thou - sands of an - gels and
F/A
G/B
N.C.
wings of ser - a - phim.
CHORUS
Cm
Gm7
A♭2
E♭
B♭/D
Cm
All glo - ry and hon - or, all
Gm7
A♭
B♭/A♭
A♭
B♭
Cm
Gm7
pow - er and praise; We join with the
A♭2
E♭
Fm
Cm7
E♭sus/A♭
an - gels, giv - ing glo - ry to Your

Medley options: I See the Lord; High and Lifted Up (CHRISTENSEN).

"To him who sits on the throne and to the Lamb be praise and honor and glory and power, for ever and ever!" Revelation 5:13 (NIV)

887

All Heaven Declares

HM-72

Words and Music by
NOEL RICHARDS and
TRICIA RICHARDS

Medley options: Jesus, We Enthrone You; I Sing Praises.

I can do everything through Him who gives me strength. Philippians 4:13 (NIV)

888 All the Power You Need

HM-68

Words and Music by
RUSSELL FRAGAR

Em
it takes faith;
Trust Him and see
He's got
C
D7
G7
all the pow'r you need.
CHORUS
C7
B♭
G7
He saves, for - gives, and heals,
takes back what the
C7
Dev - il steals;
My debt's been paid in full,
D7(+5)
and ev - 'ry day He does mir - a - cles.

VERSE
G7
I got dreams, turn them in-to plans___ too big for
3rd time to Coda
Em
hu-man___ hands;___ Trust Him and see___ He's got
C
D7
G7
all the pow'r you need.___
BRIDGE
G
He's real, He's real, faith's a lot strong-er than
what you___ feel;___ He's real, He's real,

Medley options: Call Him Up (Can't Stop Praisin'); Jesus, We Celebrate Your Victory.

…"Alleluia! For the Lord God Omnipotent reigns!" Revelation 19:6 (NKJ)

Alleluia

889

HM-70

Words and Music by
JERRY SINCLAIR

Medley options: High and Lifted Up (CHRISTENSEN); In the Presence of Jehovah.

...I am with you always, to the very end of the age. Matthew 28:20 (NIV)

890

Always

HM-69

Words and Music by
PAUL BALOCHE

F/A
Gm7
I re - joice to know that's how
B♭/C
F
B♭/F F
N.C.
You'll al - ways be.
CHORUS
C
B♭/C
F/A
B♭
Al - ways, for - ev - er and ev - er, You will be my God,
F
Gm7
C
You will al - ways be the shep - herd of my soul;
N.C.
C2/E
B♭2/D
Al - ways, for - ev - er and ev - er,

Medley options: Rejoice (BALOCHE/HARRIS); Firm Foundation.

…As for me and my house, we will serve the Lord. Joshua 24:15 (KJV)

As for Me and My House

HM-74

Words and Music by
TOM BROOKS, MARTIN J. NYSTROM
and DON HARRIS

Gm7 Am7 Dm7
low our God and o - bey His voice; From this day
B♭maj7 F2/A Gm7 B♭/C
1.
and for the rest of our lives, we will serve the Lord.
F2 Dm7 B♭maj7 F2/A Gm7 B♭/C F2 Dm7 E♭maj7 F2
We will
VERSE
B♭m7 E♭ B♭ F2/A
not bow to an - oth - er god, we will have
A♭2 B♭2 Fmaj7/C
no oth - er gods but You; We will

Medley options: Celebrate the Lord of Love; One True Living God.

...As the deer pants for streams of water, so my soul pants for you, O God. Psalm 42:1 (NIV)

892 As the Deer

HM-69

Words and Music by
MARTIN J. NYSTROM

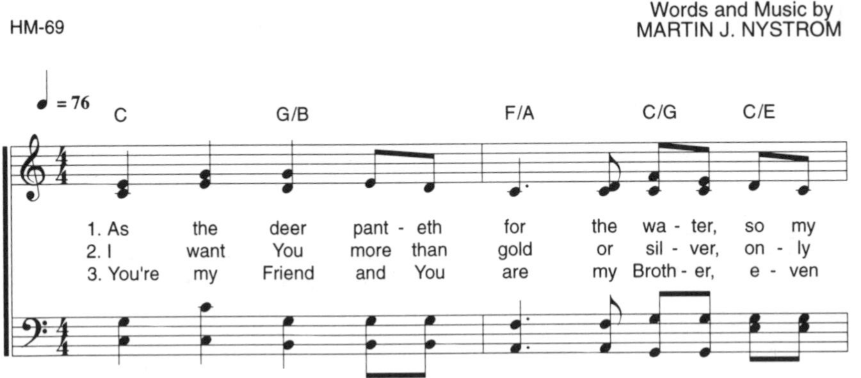

Medley options: You Are Here; More Precious Than Silver; I Worship You, Almighty God.

…The Lord your God… is a great and awesome God. Deuteronomy 7:21 (NIV)

893 Awesome God

HM-73

Words and Music by
RICH MULLINS

Medley options: Spirit of the Sovereign God; All Consuming Fire.

This righteousness from God comes through faith in Jesus Christ to all who believe… Romans 3:22 (NIV)

Can You Believe

894

HM-73

Words and Music by
ALVIN MIRANDA

Medley options: Look What the Lord Has Done; Enemy's Camp.

...In Your presence is fullness of joy, at Your right hand are pleasures forevermore. Psalm 16:11 (NKJ)

Center of My Joy

HM-74

Words and Music by
GLORIA GAITHER and
RICHARD SMALLWOOD

VERSE
C
C/E
1. When I've lost my di - rec - tion, You're the
2. You are why I find pleas - ure in the
F
C/E
Am7
C/D
Bm/D D7
com-pass for my way, You're the fire and light when nights are long and
sim - ple things in life, You're the mu-sic in the mead-ows and the
F/G
C
C/E
3
cold; Through the sad - ness, You are the laugh - ter that
streams; You're in the voic - es of my chil - dren, in my
3
F
C/E
Dm2/B
E7
shad - ows all my fears, when I'm
fam - 'ly and my home, You're the
Am7
C/D
Bm/D D7
F/G
down and out Your hand is there to hold.
source and fin - ish - er of my high - est dreams.

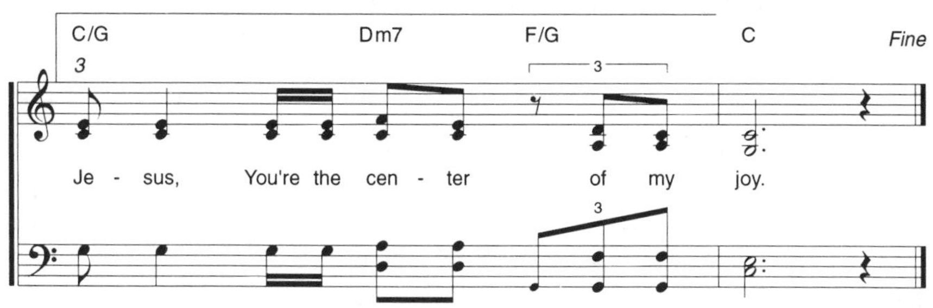

Medley options: Honor and Glory; No Other Name.

In Him we have redemption through His blood… with the riches of God's grace. Ephesians 1:7 (NIV)

896 Come Thou Fount of Every Blessing

HM-71

Words and Music by
ROBERT ROBINSON

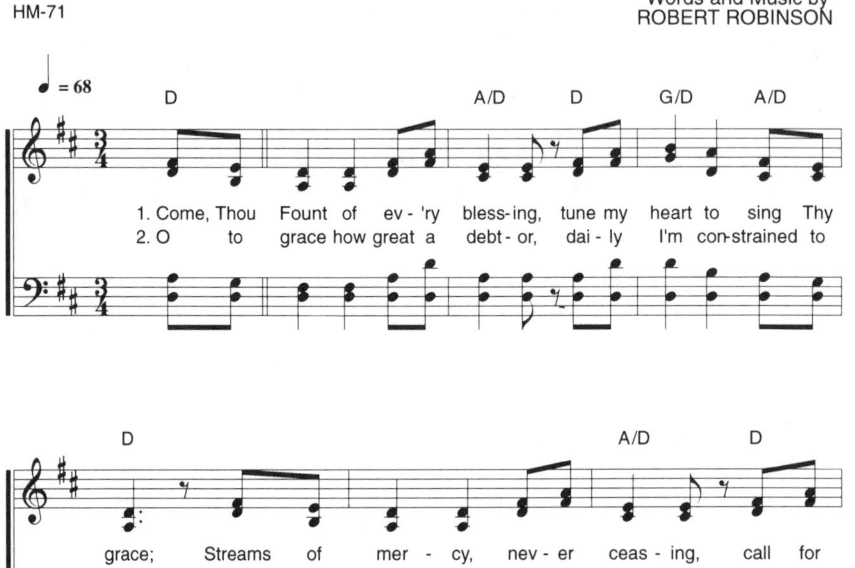

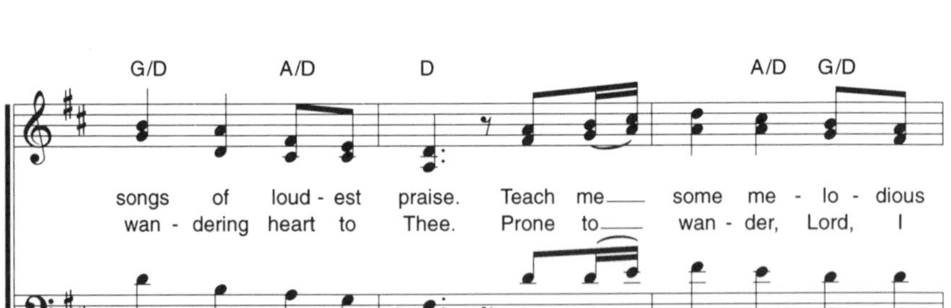

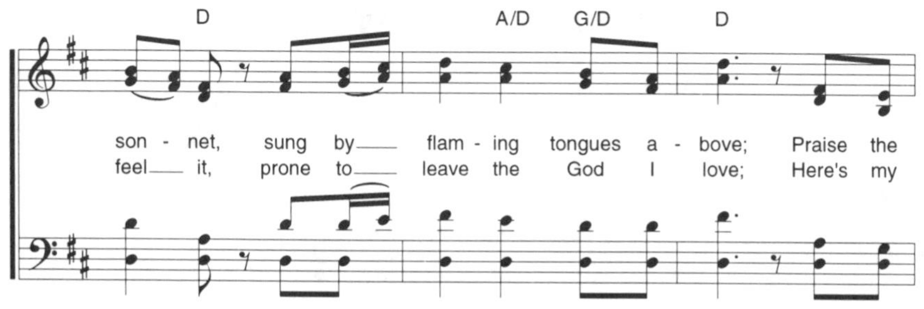

Medley options: Flow, O Mighty Holy River; I Will Come and Bow Down.

...So they said, "Let us rise up and build." Then they set their hands to this good work. Nehemiah 2:18 (NKJ)

897 Doin' a Good Work

HM-70

Words and Music by
DAVID BARONI and
KIRK HENDERSON

A m7/D
voic - es in the night, we're
viv - al to this land, then the
E♭maj7
build - ing with the left hand and we're
world will see His pow - er through His
D 7sus
D 7(+5)(♯9)
bat - tling with the right. We're
peo - ple once a - gain. We're
CHORUS
G 9
F 9
G
F 13
do- in' a good work for the king- dom of God,
G 9
D
E m7
F° D/F♯
do- in' a good work, we're gon- na stand our ground; Re-

D m7
G 9
F/G
viv - al is out - pour - ing for re -
C maj9
F9,♯11,13
build - ing and re - stor - ing, we're
B♭maj7
E7(♯9)
do - in' a work for Je - sus and we
N.C.
1.
F maj7/G
G 9
won't come, we won't come down.
N.C.
2.
F maj7/G
won't come, we won't come down.

Medley options: I Lift Up My Eyes; More than Enough.

The God of peace will soon crush Satan under your feet... Romans 16:20 (NIV)

898 Enemy's Camp

HM-73

AUTHOR UNKNOWN

Medley options: Can You Believe; Our Help Is in the Name of the Lord.

...I will praise you, O Lord, with all my heart... Psalm 9:1 (NIV)

899 Fairest Lord Jesus

Text from Munster Gesangbuch, verse two by Joseph A. Seiss

Music from Schlesische Volkslieder

HM-69

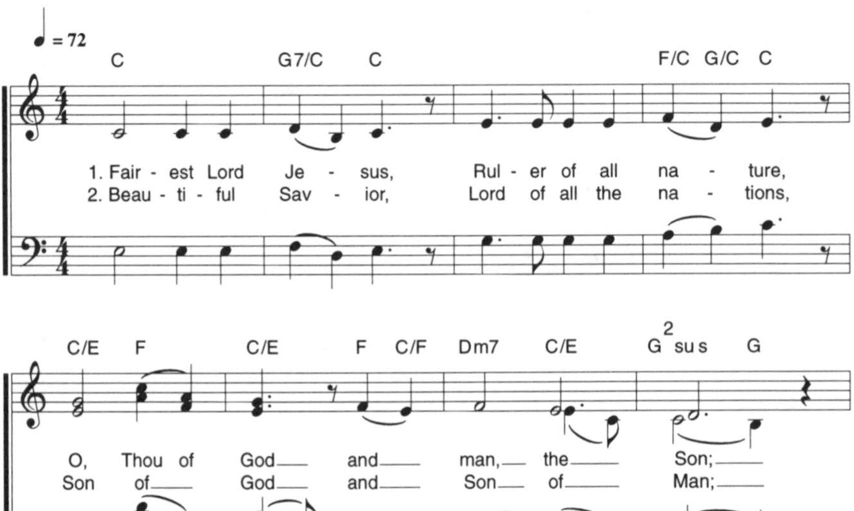

Medley options: My Jesus, I Love Thee; Jesus, We Enthrone You.

I am the resurrection and the life. He who believes in me will live… John 11:25 (NIV)

Father of Creation

900

HM-68

Words and Music by
ROBERT EASTWOOD

E
F♯m7
B
gave a life worth liv - ing, a life in love with You, and
F♯m7
B
now I just love giv - ing all my
Amaj7
E2/G♯
F♯m7
E
B/D♯
prais - es back to You. You're the
CHORUS
C♯m
G♯m7
Fa-ther of cre-a - tion, the ris - en Lamb of God, You're the
A
One who walked a - way from the

E
B/D♯
emp - ty tomb that day; And You
C♯m
set Your peo - ple free with
G♯m7
A2
love and lib - er - ty, and I can walk with You ev - 'ry
Bsus
1.
B
night and ev - 'ry day. We
Bsus
2.
B
B/D♯
D.S.
night and ev - 'ry day. You're the

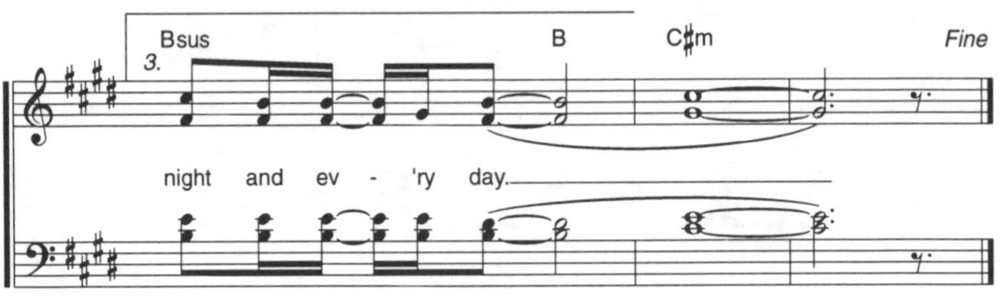

Medley options: Blessed Be the Lord God Almighty (FITTS);
Exalt the Lord Our God (GARDNER).

No weapon formed against you shall prosper, and every tongue
which rises against you in judgment You shall condemn. Isaiah 54:17 (NKJ)

Go Ahead

HM-74

Words and Music by
RON KENOLY

Fm
If you catch___ hell___ don't hold it, if you're
Great - er is He___ that is in you than
B♭m
Fm
go - ing through hell___ don't stop.
He___ that's in___ the world.
If you catch___ hell___ don't hold it, if you're
Great - er is He___ that is in you than
B♭m
Fm
go - ing through hell___ don't stop. Re - mem - ber,
He___ that's in___ the world. Re - mem - ber,
Fm
no weap - on formed a - gainst you shall pros - per,___

eve - ry tongue that ris - es a - gainst you,
B♭m
Fm
you shall con - demn. Re - mem - ber,
no weap - on formed a - gainst you shall pros - per,
B♭m
Fm
1.
eve - ry tongue that ris - es a - gainst you,
you shall con - demn.
B♭m
Fm
2.
you shall con - demn.
Go a -
Go - in'

N. C.
head, go a - head, go a -
through, go - in' through, go - in'
head, go a - head, go a - head. Go a -
through, go - in' through, go - in' through. Go - in'
head, go a - head, go a -
through, go - in' through, go - in'
1.
head, go a - head, go a - head. Go - in
2.
through, go - in through, go - in through. You have au -

Fm7
Bbm7
Db
thor - i - ty over the en - e - my, you have au -
Fm
Db
Gm11
Bb/C
thor - i - ty as a be - liev - er; You have au -
Fm7
Bbm7
Db
thor - i - ty over the en - e - my, you have au -
Fm
Db
Gm11
Bb/C
thor - i - ty in the name of Je - sus.
Fm
If you catch hell don't hold it, if you're

B♭m
Fm
go - ing through hell don't stop.
If you catch hell don't hold it, if you're
B♭m
Fm
go - ing through hell don't stop.
If you catch hell don't hold it, if you're
B♭m
Fm
go - ing through hell don't stop.

Medley options: Romans 16:19; The Solid Rock (HARRIS).

Now to Him who is able to do exceedingly abundantly above all that we ask or think…
to Him be glory… Ephesians 3:20,21 (NKJ)

902

God Can

HM-70

Words and Music by
GERON DAVIS and
NANCY GORDON

A♭2/C
E♭/B♭
F9
B♭9
to the light of day, God can,
wipe a - way your tears, God can,
make a brand new start, God can,
E♭9
God can. God can
God can. God can
God can. God can
CHORUS
A♭
A♭/C
A♭/E♭ E♭
Cm7
do more than you could ev - er ask or think, He
B♭9
E♭
D/E♭ D♭/E♭ E♭7
holds all pow - er in His might - y hand; When

A♭
Fm7
B♭
you can't see your way,___ just re - mem -
E♭
E♭/G
A♭
F9
B♭9
ber this,__ my friend,___ God can,___ God can.___
E♭
1,2.
A♭/B♭
2,3. When
E♭
3.
B♭/D Cm7
When
BRIDGE 1
B♭
E♭
you are at__ your weak - est, He'll fill you with__ His strength;__ It's
B♭
E♭
not by might,__ but by His Spir - it that we do__ all things.__

A♭
E♭
You can face the future when your hope is in His
A♭
hands.
God can
CHORUS
A
A/C♯
A/E E
C♯m7
do more than you could ev - er ask or think, He
B 9
E
E♭/E D/E E 7
holds all pow - er in His might - y hand; When
A
F♯m7
B
you can't see your way, just re - mem -

E
E/G♯
A
F♯9
B9
ber this, my friend, God can, God can.
BRIDGE 2
E2/G♯
C♯m11
F♯m11
B
B/D♯
I have a God, Who can
E2
Bsus/G♯
C♯m11
F♯m11
B
B/D♯
do an-y-thing, I have a God, Who is
E2
Bsus/G♯
C♯m11
F♯m11
B
B/D♯
still King of kings; I have a God, Who is
E2
Bsus/G♯
C♯7(♯9)
F♯9
a-ble to do a-bove and be-yond what you could

Medley options: More than Enough; Hosanna (SPRINGER/WILLIAMSON).

The Lord is my strength and my song; he has become my salvation... Exodus 15:2 (NIV)

903 God Gives His Children a Song

HM-70

Words and Music by
ALVIN SLAUGHTER

C/D
G2
throne.
But then Ad - am fell in the gar -
done.
Yet, they lift - ed their voic - es in prais -
F2
C2/E
den,
old Sa - tan thought He'd won the vic - to -
es,
the chains that they wore came un -
G2/D
C2
ry;
Then Je - sus came all the way from
done;
For God sent a strong and might - y
G2/B
Em7
Am7
C/D
glo - ry
just to give us a rea - son to
shak - ing,
there's vic - to - ry when you sing a
G2
sing.
Sing, "hal - le -
song.
Sing, "hal - le -

CHORUS
Bm7 Em7 Am7 C/D G
lu - jah!" He's the joy of my salvation, halle -
Bm7 Em7 Am7 C/D G
lu - jah, glo - ry to the Ho - ly One; Halle -
Bm7 E7 Am Bm7 E7 Asus Am
lu - jah, ev - 'ry tongue and ev - 'ry na - tion, my
Am7 G/B C6 C/D Am/D D/F♯ G Em7
God gives His chil - dren a song,
Am7 G/B C6 C/D Am/D D/F♯ G
1.
God gives His chil - dren a song.

C/D
2.
2. In a
VERSE
C/D
G2
3. When you're
bur - dened and filled up with
F2
C2/E
sad - ness,
You're
long - ing to find sweet re -
G/D
C2
lief;
Just re - mem - ber there's pow - er in our
Bm7
Em7
Am7
C/D
prais - es,
ev - 'ry
dev - il in Hell's got to

CHORUS

G B m7 E m7

flee. Sing, "hal - le - lu - jah!" He's the

A m7 C/D G B m7 E m7

joy of my___ sal - va - tion, hal - le - lu - jah, glo - ry

A m7 C/D G B m7 E 7 A m

to the Ho - ly One;__ Hal - le - lu - jah, ev - 'ry

B m7 E 7 A sus A m A m7 G/B C 6 C/D A m/D D/F♯ G

tongue and ev - 'ry na - tion, my God gives__ His chil - dren__ a song,___

E m7 A m7 G/B C 6 C/D A m/D D/F♯ G E m7

___ God gives__ His chil - dren___ a song,______

Worship Leader
Well, I'm
Am7 G/B C6 C/D Am/D D/F♯ G
God gives His chil - dren a song.
BRIDGE
sing - in', sing - in', I'm
N.C. Fmaj7 Em7 N.C. Fmaj7 Em7
Congregation
I'm sing - in', I'm sing - in'.
shout - in', shout - in',
N.C. Fmaj7 Em7 N.C. Fmaj7 Em7
I'm shout - in', I'm shout - in'.

danc - in',
danc - in,
N.C.
Fmaj7 Em7
N.C.
Fmaj7 Em7
I'm danc - in',
I'm danc - in',
1.
danc - in,
danc - in,
N.C.
Fmaj7 Em7
N.C.
Fmaj7 Em7
1.
I'm danc - in',
I'm danc - in',
2.
danc - in,
danc - in'.
N.C.
Fmaj7
Em7
G
2.
I'm danc - in'. I'm sing - in', "hal - le -

CHORUS
Bm7 Em7 Am7 C/D G
lu - jah!" He's the joy of my sal - va - tion, hal - le -
Bm7 Em7 Am7 C/D G
lu - jah, glo - ry to the Ho - ly One; Hal - le -
Bm7 E7 Am Bm7 E7 Asus Am
lu - jah, ev - 'ry tongue and ev - 'ry na - tion, my
Am7 G/B C6 C/D Am/D D/F♯ G Em7
God gives His chil - dren a song,
Am7 G/B C6 C/D Am/D B/D♯ Em Em7
God gives His chil - dren a song,

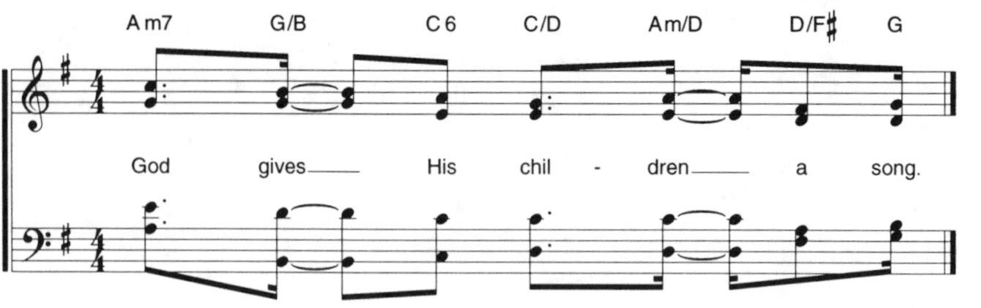

Medley options: Our Help Is in the Name of the Lord; What a Refuge.

For great is your love toward me. Psalm 86:13 (NIV)

Great Is Your Love

904

Em7 D/E Em11 G/A D/A A7sus A
to - wards me, to - wards me.
to - wards me, to - wards me.
CHORUS
Gmaj7 F♯m7 D/F♯ Em7 A7sus
You are my por - tion, both now and ev - er - more,
You are my por - tion, both now and ev - er - more,
D C♯m11 F♯7 Bm7 D/E E
I de-clare my love to You;
I de-clare my love to You;
A7sus A7 G/A A Gmaj7
My heart has been cap -
My heart has been cap -
F♯m7 D/F♯ F♯7sus F♯7 Bm7
tured by the great-ness of Your love, O, I
tured by the great-ness of Your grace, O, I

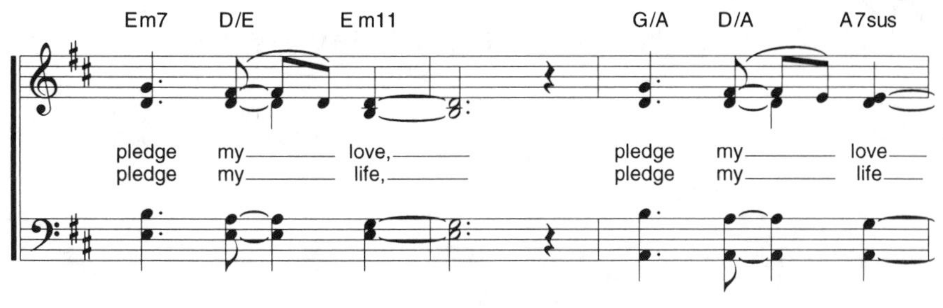

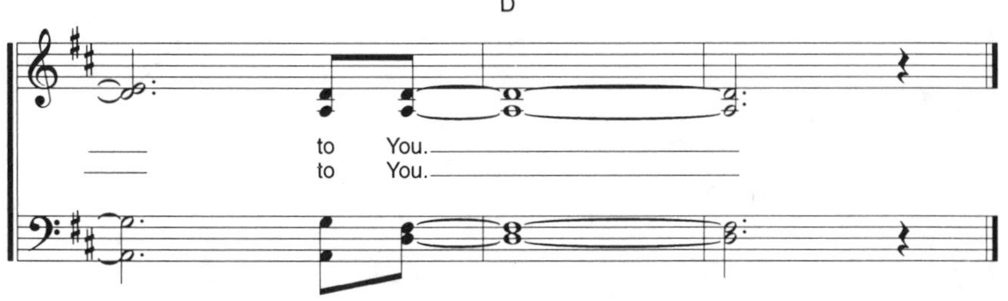

Medley options: Rest in Your Love; You Are Good.

…Do not be afraid… declares the Lord, for I am with you and will save you… Jeremiah 42:11 (NIV)

905 He Will Come and Save You

HM-71

Words and Music by
BOB FITTS and GARY SADLER

VERSE

E B C♯m A

1. Say to those who are fear - ful heart - ed,
2. Say to those who are bro - ken - heart - ed,

E B A

"do not be a - fraid";
"do not lose your faith";

E B C♯m A

The Lord, your God, is strong with His might - y arms.
The Lord, your God, is strong with His lov - ing arms.

E/G♯ B A

When you call on His name;
When you call on His name;

B
E
A2/E
E
He will come and save.
He will come and
He will come and save.
He will come and
CHORUS
A
B
E
E/G♯
A
B
save you,
He will come and
save you;
C♯m
A
E/B
Say to the wear - y one,
"your God will sure -
B
E/G♯
A
Bsus
B
ly come,"
He will come and
save you.
E
A
B
E
E/G♯
He will come and
save you,
He will come and

A
B
C♯m
save you; Lift up your eyes
A
E/B
B
E/G♯
to Him, you will a - rise a - gain, He will come and
1.
A
Bsus
B
A
save you.
2.
A
Bsus
B
E
save you.
BRIDGE
C♯m
B/D♯
He is our ref - uge in the day of troub - le,
E
F♯m7
E/G♯
He is our shel - ter in the time of storm;
He is our tow - er in the

Medley options: More of You; Only Jesus; Extol the Name.

If my people, who are called by my name, will humble themselves and pray…
then will I…heal their land. 2 Chronicles 7:14 (NIV)

906

Heal Their Land

HM-74

Words and Music by
RON KENOLY

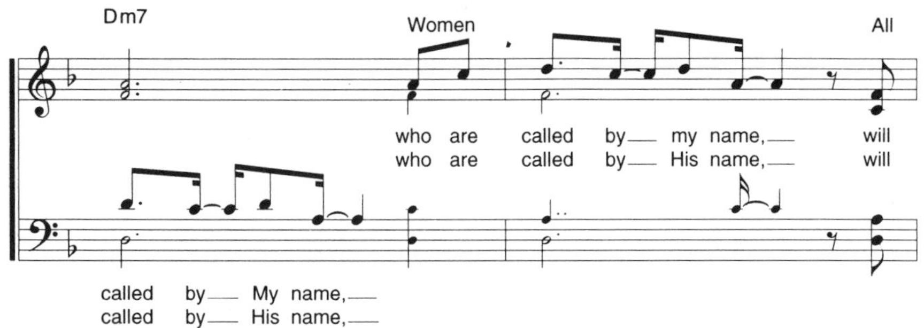
Dm7
Women
All
who are called by my name, will
who are called by His name, will
called by My name,
called by His name,

Gm7
C2
C/D
hum - ble them - selves and pray, and
hum - ble them - selves and pray, and

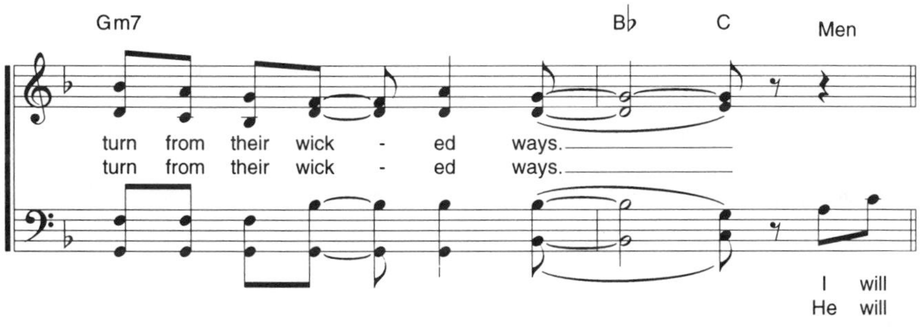
Gm7
B♭
C
Men
turn from their wick - ed ways.
turn from their wick - ed ways.
I will
He will

VERSE

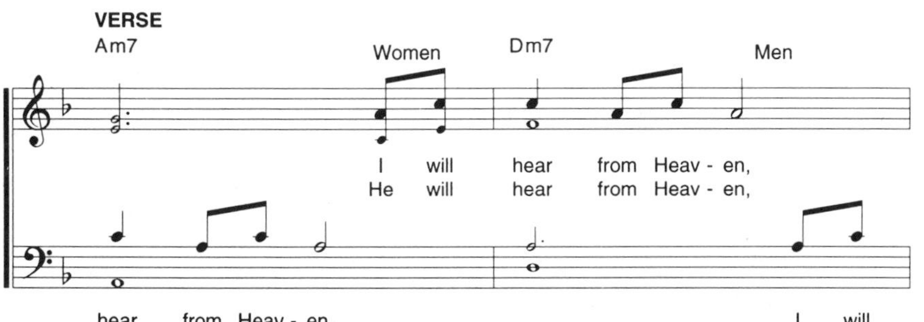
Am7
Women
Dm7
Men
I will hear from Heav - en,
He will hear from Heav - en,
hear from Heav - en, I will
hear from Heav - en, He will

Medley options: God Is Able (ROGERS); Let Everything That Has Breath (GOMEZ).

…"If only I may touch His garment, I shall be made well." Matthew 9:21 (NKJ)

He's All I Need

907

HM-70

Author unknown

Medley options: Be It unto Me; Blessed Be the Name of the Lord.

…I saw the Lord seated on a throne, high and exalted, and the train of his robe filled the temple. Isaiah 6:1 (NIV)

908 High and Exalted

HM-71

Words and Music by
KYLE RASMUSSEN

Medley options: We Lift You High; I Stand in Awe; In the Presence.

…Holy, holy, holy is the Lord Almighty; the whole earth is full of his glory." Isaiah 6:3 (NIV)

909

Holy, Holy, Holy

HM-73

Words and Music by
REGINALD HEBER & JOHN DYKES

♩ = 58

D Bm7 A D/F♯ G G+ Em/G

1. Ho - ly, ho - ly, ho - ly! Lord God Al -
2. Ho - ly, ho - ly, ho - ly! all the saints a -
3. Ho - ly, ho - ly, ho - ly! though the dark - ness
4. Ho - ly, ho - ly, ho - ly! Lord God Al -

D/F♯ D A/C♯ D A/C♯ Bm E/G♯ A D

might - y! Ear - ly in the morn - ing our
dore Thee, cast - ing down their gold - en crowns a -
hide Thee, though the eye of sin - ful man Thy
might - y! All Thy works shall praise Thy name in

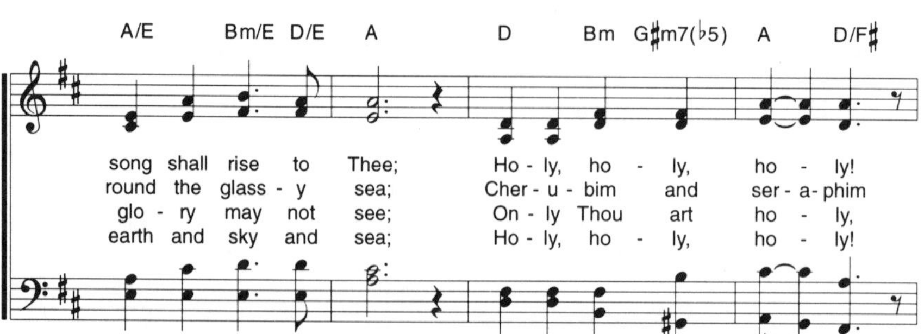

Medley options: O Lord, You're Beautiful; Anointing Fall on Me.

…"Holy, holy, holy is the Lord God Almighty…" Revelation 4:8 (NIV)

910

Holy, Holy, Holy

HM-70

Words and Music by
GARY OLIVER

Fm/E♭ E♭ Fm/E♭ E♭
Gm7 A♭ E♭/G
wor - thy to re - ceive hon - or, wor - thy to re - ceive
Fm7 E♭ B♭7 A♭/B♭ E♭
all our praise to - day.
CHORUS
D♭/E♭ A♭/E♭ D♭/E♭ A♭/E♭ E♭
Praise Him, praise Him and lift Him up;
N.C. D♭/E♭ A♭/E♭
Praise Him, ex -
D♭/E♭ A♭/E♭ E♭ D♭/E♭ A♭/E♭
alt His name for - ev - er. Praise Him,

Medley options: Glorious God; No Eye Has Seen (CHISUM/TAYLOR).

…"Holy, holy, holy is the Lord Almighty, the whole earth is full of his glory." Isaiah 6:3

Holy Is the Lord

911

HM-71

Words and Music by
LYNN DeSHAZO

Medley options: Lord, I Thirst for You; We Worship You.

For where two or three come together in my name, there am I with them… Matthew 18:20 (NIV)

I Believe the Presence

912

HM-68

Words and Music by
RUSSELL FRAGAR

E♭m/B♭
B♭
Dm7 Gm7
ple have come in faith; There's a might-
Cm9
y sound and a touch of fire when we're
F
gath - ered in one place.
CHORUS
B♭ D7(♭5) Gm7
Fm
E♭
B♭
I be - lieve that the pres - ence of God is here;
Dm7
Gm7
Cm9
There's not one thing that can't be changed when the Spir -

E♭ E♭/F B♭ D7(♭5) Gm7 Fm
it of God is near. I be - lieve that the pres - ence of
E♭ B♭ Cm9 Dm7
God is here; When two or three are gath -
Gm7 Dm7(♭5) Cm9 Dm7
ered, when peo - ple rise in faith,
Gm7 Dm7(♭5) Cm9 Dm7
I be - lieve God an -
last time to Coda
Gm7 Dm7(♭5) Cm9 E♭/F F7
swers, and His pres- ence is in this place.

A♭/B♭
A/B
A♭/B♭
1.
2.
No thing on earth or heav - en
G♭/A♭
G/A
A♭/B♭
can stop the pow'r of God,
in - to our
A/B
B♭/C
hand is giv - en
the call to take it on;
No o - cean can con - tain it,
no star can
A♭/B♭
A/B
B♭/C
rise a - bove,
in - to our hearts are giv - en

Medley options: Arise Shine (RITA BALOCHE/HARVILL);
Be Bold, Be Strong (CHAPMAN); Celebrate Jesus

I can do all things through Christ which strengtheneth me. Philippians 4:13 (KJV)

913 I Can Do All Things

HM-71

Words and Music by
PAUL BALOCHE
and DON HARRIS

Medley options: The Spirit of the Lord; Glory, Glory Lord.

I love you, O Lord, my strength. Psalm 18:1 (NIV)

914 I Love to Love You, Lord

Words and Music by
RON KENOLY and
LOUIS SMITH

HM-74

Am
D/F♯
G
C/E
Spir - it and Your grace,
I'm
goal and my de - sire
is to
F2
F
C
Am
D/F♯
con - fi - dent You'll solve them.
I'm
serve and give You rev - 'rence.
I'm
CHORUS
G
G/B
C
Am
D/F♯
G
G/B
F/A
G/B
here to say, "I love You," I'm here to say, "I a-
C
Am
D/F♯
G
G/B
Am
Em
Am
dore You"; I'm here to say, "I love You," I
Dm9
F/G
G
C
G/B
Am
Em
Dm9
F/G
G
love to love You, Lord, I love to love You,

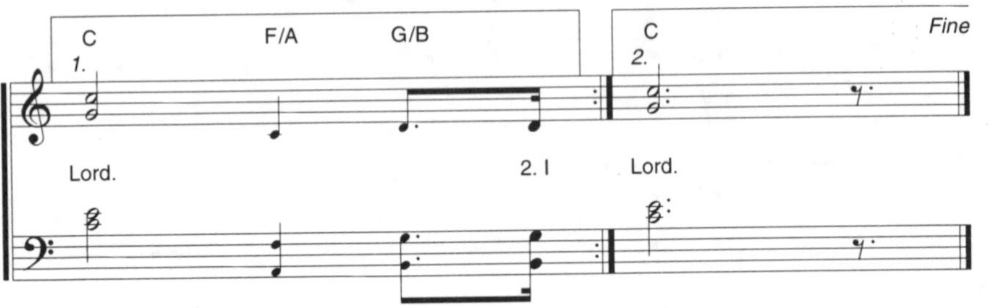

Medley options: Rest in Your Love; I Love to Be with You.

...I love you, O Lord, my strength. Psalm 18:1 (NIV)

I Love You, Lord

915

HM-70

Words and Music by
LAURIE KLEIN

Medley options: I Want to Be Where You Are; I Worship You, Almighty God.

As the deer pants for streams of water, so my soul pants for you, O God. Psalm 42:1 (NIV)

I Need You More

HM-73

Words and Music by
LINDELL COOLEY & BRUCE HAYNES

VERSE
A♭2
B♭
Cm
I breathe, more than the song I sing;
E♭/G
A♭2
More than the next heart - beat,
Fm/E♭
E♭
E♭/G
more than an - y - thing. And Lord, as time
A♭2
B♭
Cm
goes by, I'll be by Your side;
Fm
E♭/G
'Cause I nev - er want to go back to

Medley options: I Want to Be More Like You; More Than Anything (CHRISTENSEN).

How great is Your goodness, which You have stored up for those who fear You… Psalm 31:19 (NIV)

917 I Testify Today

HM-74

Words and Music by
RON KENOLY and
LOUIS SMITH

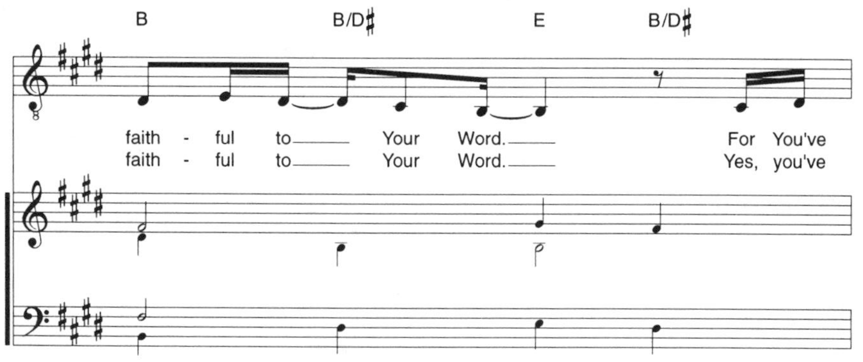
B
B/D♯
E
B/D♯
faith - ful to Your Word. For You've
faith - ful to Your Word. Yes, you've

C♯m2
F♯m7
B2
Emaj7
been so ver - y good to me, I'm Yours ex - clu - sive - ly,
been so ver - y good to me, You've made my life com - plete,

Amaj7
F♯m7
Dmaj7
Bsus
B
that's why I tes - ti - fy to - day.
that's why I tes - ti - fy to - day.

CHORUS
C♯m
C♯/E♯
F♯m2
F♯m(+7) F♯m7
1.
I'm Yours, Lord, I'm Yours, I'm

A/B
B/D♯
E
G♯7sus/D♯ G♯7
Yours, Lord, I'm Yours; For You've

C♯m
F♯m7
B2
Emaj7
been so ver - y good to me, I'm Yours ex - clu - sive- ly,

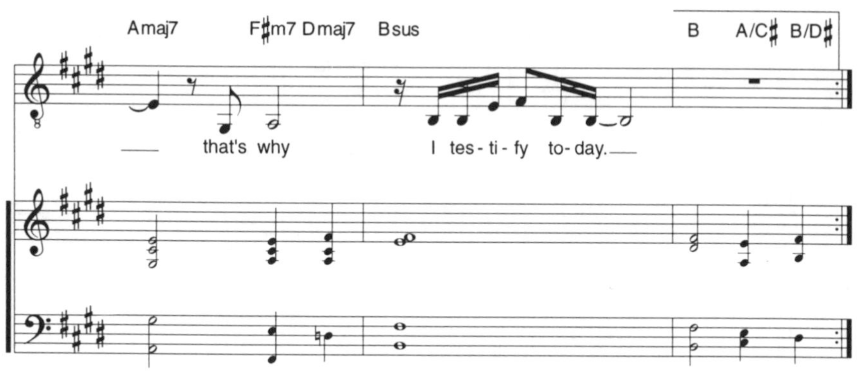
Amaj7
F♯m7 Dmaj7
Bsus
B
A/C♯
B/D♯
that's why
I tes - ti - fy to - day.

CHORUS

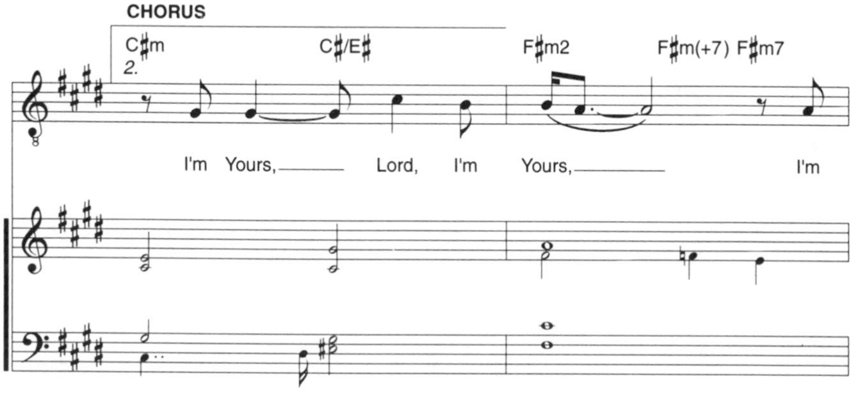
C♯m
2.
C♯/E♯
F♯m2
F♯m(+7) F♯m7
I'm Yours,
Lord, I'm
Yours,
I'm

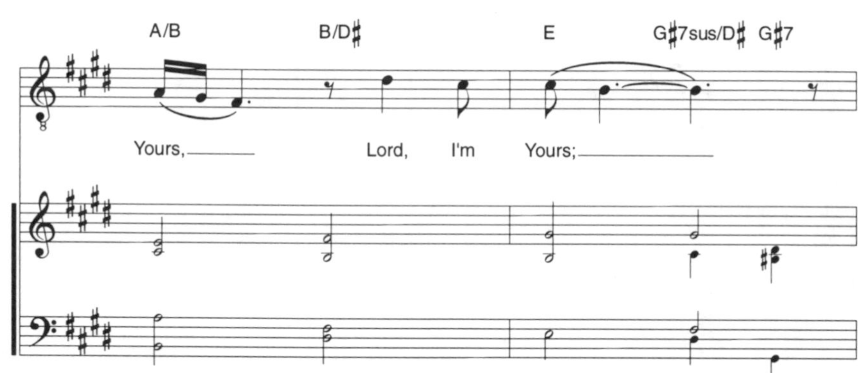
A/B
B/D♯
E
G♯7sus/D♯ G♯7
Yours,
Lord, I'm
Yours;

C♯m
C♯/E♯
F♯m2
F♯m(+7)
F♯m7
I'm Yours, all my heart, my soul, my mind, my life is

A/B
B
B♯○
C♯m
C♯/E♯
Yours. I'm Yours, Lord, I'm

F♯m2
F♯m(+7)
F♯m7
A/B
B/D♯
Yours, I'm Yours, Lord, I'm

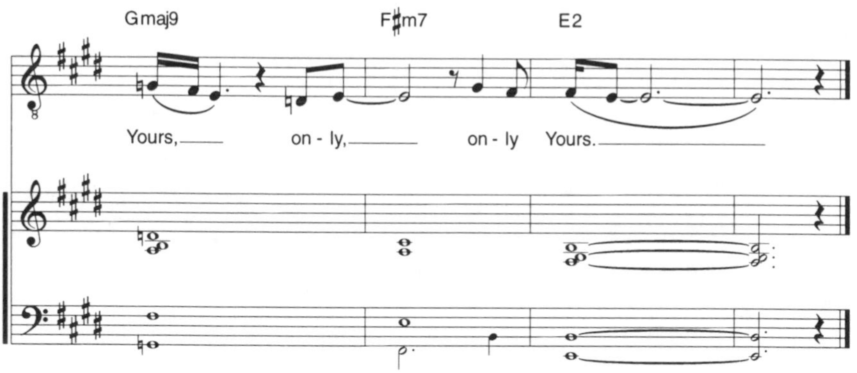

Medley options: More Than Anything (CHRISTENSEN); I Need You More.

Praise him with the timbrel and dance; praise him with stringed instruments and organs. Psalm 150:4 (KJV)

918 I Will Dance

HM-74

Words and Music by
KIRK WILLIAMS

♩ = 116

CHORUS

G   Am/G
In the morn - ing, when ___ I rise, ___ I will

G   Am/G   D/G G
lift up ___ my eyes ___ and be - hold, I ___ will dance. ___

Am/G   G   Am/G
In the morn - ing, when ___ I rise, ___ I will

Fmaj7/G   G   Am/G   D/G G
lift up ___ my eyes ___ and be - hold, I ___ will dance. ___

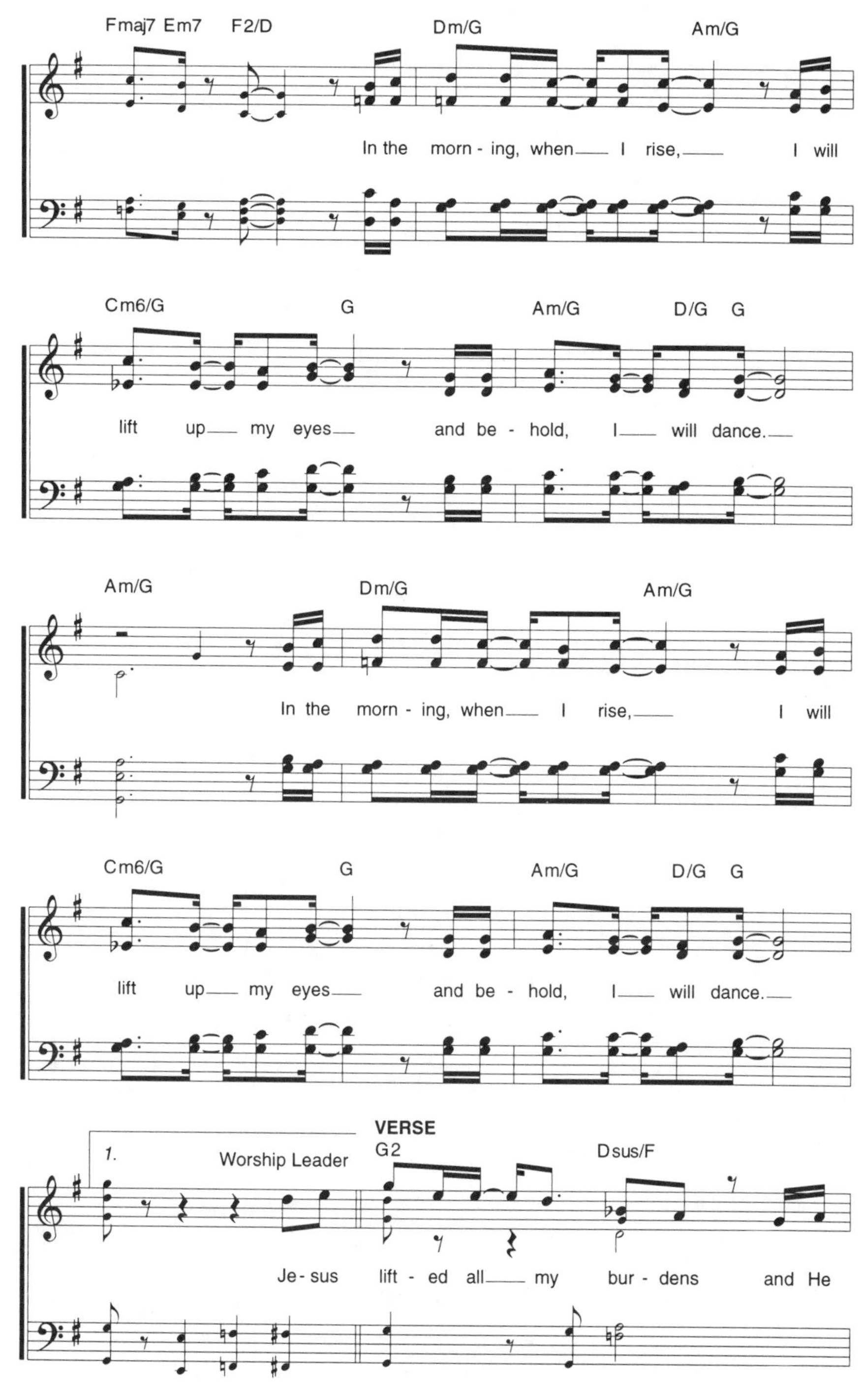
Fmaj7 Em7 F2/D
Dm/G
Am/G
In the morn - ing, when I rise, I will
Cm6/G
G
Am/G
D/G G
lift up my eyes and be - hold, I will dance.
Am/G
Dm/G
Am/G
In the morn - ing, when I rise, I will
Cm6/G
G
Am/G
D/G G
lift up my eyes and be - hold, I will dance.
VERSE
1.
Worship Leader
G2
Dsus/F
Je - sus lift - ed all my bur - dens and He

All
Worship Leader
Em11 F2/D G Am/G G
washed all my sins a - way, a - way; And then He
G2 Dsus/F Em11 F2/D
took this earth - en bod - y and He made it His dwell - ing
G Am/G G All 2. Worship Leader
place. In the Je - sus
VERSE
G2 Dsus/F Em11 F2/D G All Am/G
lift - ed all my bur - dens He washed all my sins a - way, a -
Worship Leader
G G2 Dsus/F
way; And then He took this earth - en bod - y He

Em11 F2/D G Am/G
made it His dwell - ing place.
G G2 Dsus/F
He said He would nev- er leave me or for- sake me,
All Worship Leader
Em11 F2/D G Am/G G
be with me through thick and thin, and thin; So, I have
F2 C2/E Dm7 Fmaj7
o- pened up my heart and let the beau- ty of His love come
All
G Fmaj7 Em7 Dm7 C B♭6 Am7
3.
in. In the Let's

BRIDGE
G2
sing, let's dance, let's cel - e - brate, to -
F2/D
geth - er, let's praise the Lord; Let's
G2
sing, let's dance, let's cel - e - brate, eve - ry -
F2/D
1st x only
bod - y make a joy - ful noise. Let's

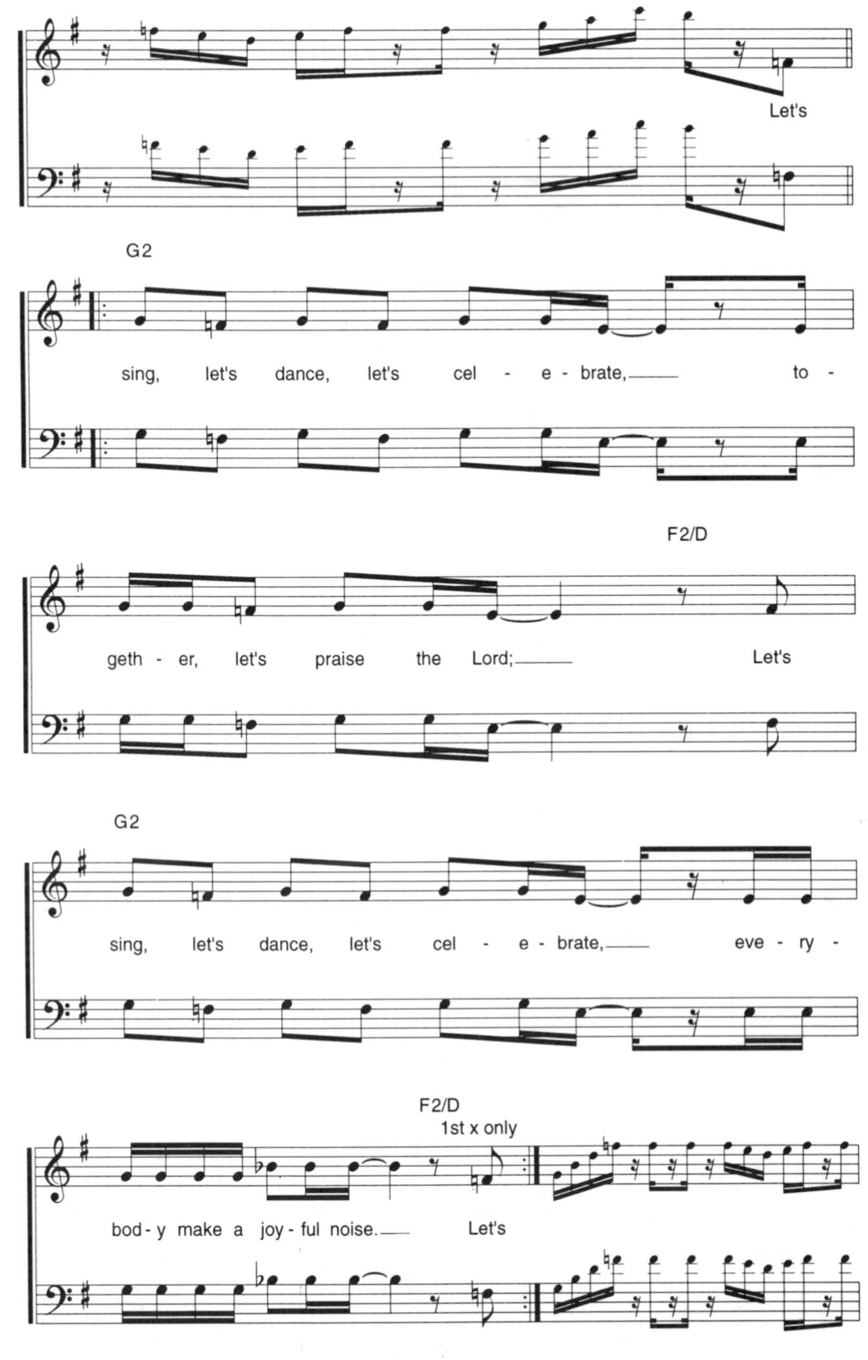

Let's
G2
sing, let's dance, let's cel - e - brate, to -
F2/D
geth - er, let's praise the Lord; Let's
G2
sing, let's dance, let's cel - e - brate, eve - ry -
F2/D
1st x only
bod - y make a joy - ful noise. Let's

Worship Leader: in a rap!
Our God is good, my God is great, if you
give me just a min - ute I'll e - lab - o - rate. I got a
new heart, a new life, re - gen - er - at - ed mind and a
fu - ture with Him that can't be meas - ured by time. I'm gon - na

hang with Him for the rest of my days, as
long as I can speak, I'm gon - na give Him praise. So, get up
with me and get in - to this thing, put your
3
All: Shouted!
G2
Dsus/F
Em11
hands in the air, give it up for the King! Hal - le - lu -
F2/D G2 Dsus/F Em11 F2/D G2 Dsus/F Em11
jah! Hal - le - lu - jah! Hal - le - lu -

F2/D G2 Dsus/F Em11 1. F2/D G2
jah! Hal - le - lu - jah! Hal -
2. F2/D
CHORUS
G Am/G
- jah! In the morn - ing, when I rise, I will
G Am/G D/G G
lift up my eyes and be - hold, I will dance.
Am/G G Am/G
In the morn - ing, when I rise, I will
Fmaj7/G G Am/G D/G G
lift up my eyes and be - hold, I will dance.

Medley options: Ain't Gonna Let No Rock; Mourning into Dancing;
Put Your Hands Together.

You are my God, and I will give you thanks. Psalm 118:28 (NIV)

919 I Will Give You Thanks

HM-72

Words and Music by
MARTIN F. BALL

C Am D Bm Em Am D
You I a - dore, King of kings, Lord of lords.
CHORUS
G/B C G/C D D/C G/B C G/C D D/C G/B C G/C
I wor- ship You, I wor- ship You. I wor- ship
D C G/B C D7sus C G/B
1. 2.
You, I wor - ship You. You.
Am7 G/B C Am D Bm Em Am D
It is You I a- dore, King of kings, Lord of lords.
CHORUS
G/B C G/C D D/C G/B C G/C D D/C G/B C G/C
I wor- ship You! I wor- ship You! I wor- ship

Medley options: Be Magnified; We Lift You High.

He saved them from the hand of the foe; from the hand of the enemy he redeemed them. Psalm 106:10 (NIV)

920 I Will Never Be

HM-68

Words and Music by
GEOFF BULLOCK

♩ = 76

VERSE 1

D G/D G/B A/C♯ D D/F♯
I will nev - er be___ the same a - gain,___

G A G/B A/C♯ D Dsus/A
I can nev - er re - turn,___ I've closed the door;___

D G/D G/B A/C♯ D D/F♯
I will walk the path,___ I'll run the race,___ and I___

G A G/B A/C♯ D
___ will nev - er___ be the same a - gain.___

CHORUS
C G/B Asus A/C♯ D
Fall like fire, soak like rain,
C G/B Asus A/C♯ D D/C
flow like might - y wa - ters, a - gain and a - gain;
B♭ C/B♭
Sweep a - way the dark - - - ness,
Am7 D/A Em7 D/F♯
burn a - way the chaff, and let a flame burn to
G A
glo - ri - fy Your name.

Medley options: Let the Flame Burn Brighter; Salvation Belongs to Our God.

Come, let us bow down in worship… Psalm 95:6 (NIV)

I Worship You

921

B♭ F/A
o - pen up___ my eyes, Lord to
Gm7 F/B♭ Dm Csus C
see Your glo - ry.___
CHORUS
F/A B♭ Gm7 Csus C C/B♭ F/A B♭ B♭maj7/D
Je - sus, joy of my de - sire,___ You have set my heart on
Csus C Dm Fmaj7/C B♭ F/A A/C♯
fire;___ On - ly You a - lone___ can sat - is - fy,___ pour Your
Dm Fmaj7/C B♭ F/A Gm7 Csus C
love up - on___ this heart___ of mine.___ I want more of You,___

Medley options: Pure in Heart; Lord, We Welcome You.

My soul thirsts for God, for the living God… Psalm 42:2 (NIV)

922 Jesus Is Everything I Need

HM-70

Words and Music by
WAYNE GOODINE

Medley options: He's All I Need; Amazing Grace.

But You are a shield around me, O Lord; You bestow glory on me and lift up my head. Psalm 3:3 (NIV)

923 Jesus, Jesus

HM-68

Words and Music by
GEOFF BULLOCK

♩ = 112

VERSE 1

E♭ A♭/E♭ Fm/E♭ E♭ A♭/E♭ Fm/E♭

Je - sus, Je - sus, one

B♭ Fm7 E♭ A♭/E♭ Fm/E♭

touch of Your hand, I am healed and I am whole;

E♭ A♭/E♭ Fm/E♭ E♭ A♭/E♭ Fm/E♭ E♭

Je - sus, Je -

A♭/E♭ Fm/E♭ B♭

sus, one glimpse of Your face brings

Fm7 E♭ A♭/E♭ Fm/E♭ E♭ A♭/E♭ E♭/G
fire to my soul. And
CHORUS
B♭ Fm7 E♭ A♭/E♭ Fm/E♭ E♭ A♭/E♭ E♭
Je - sus, I come, be-
B♭ Fm7
hold - ing Your face, I am changed from glo - ry to
Fm/E♭ E♭ A♭/E♭ E♭ B♭m7/D♭ A♭/C
glo - ry; And now I see, and now I
B♭m7/D♭ A♭/C B♭
know, one touch of Your life brings

Fm7
E♭
A♭/E♭
Fm/E♭
E♭
A♭/E♭
Fm/E♭
glo - ry to my soul.
VERSE 2
E♭
A♭/E♭
Fm/E♭
E♭
A♭/E♭
Fm/E♭
Je - sus, Je - - sus, from
B♭
Fm7
E♭
A♭/E♭
Fm/E♭
dark-ness to light my life o - ver-flows;
E♭
A♭/E♭
Fm/E♭
E♭
A♭/E♭
Fm/E♭
Je - - - sus,
E♭
A♭/E♭
Fm/E♭
Je - - - - - - sus, Your

Medley options: We Lift Up Your Name; He Shall Reign.

Also we have come to believe and know that you are the Christ, the Son of the living God. John 6:69 (NKJ)

Jesus, Lord to Me

HM-70

Words and Music by
GREG NELSON and
GARY McSPADDEN

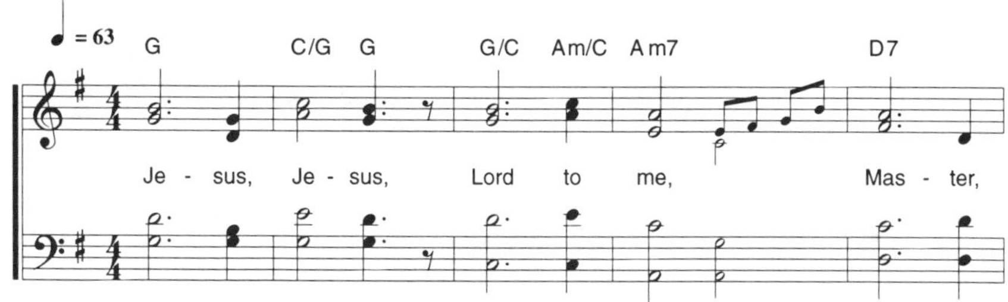

Medley options: I Look to You; Lord, I Thirst for You.

He lifted me… out of the mud and mire; he set my feet on a rock and gave me a firm place to stand. Psalm 40:2 (NIV)

925 Jesus, Lover of My Soul

HM-68

Words and Music by
JOHN EZZY, DANIEL GRUL
and STEPHEN McPHERSON

Medley options: Amazing Love; I Will Sing (ROGERS/WILLARD).

And the peace of God, which transcends all understanding, will guard your hearts and your minds in Christ Jesus. Philippians 4:7 (NIV)

926

Let the Peace of God Reign

HM-68

Words and Music by
DARLENE ZSCHECH

Medley options: Blessed Be the Lord God Almighty (BARONI);
I Worship You (BALOCHE/SADLER).

Then Jesus said, "Did I not tell you that if you believed, you would see the glory of God"? John 11:40 (NIV)

927 Look and See the Glory of the King

HM-72

Words and Music by
MARTIN F. BALL

Medley options: Majesty; Crown Him King of Kings.

The Lord has done great things for us, and we are filled with joy. Psalm 126:3 (NIV)

928 Look What the Lord Has Done

HM-73

Words and Music by
MARK DAVID HANBY

Medley options: Ain't Gonna Let No Rock; Can You Believe.

I will praise the name of God with a song, and will magnify him with thanksgiving. Psalm 69:30 (KJV)

929 Lord, I Magnify

HM-74

Words and Music by
TAVITA KENOLY

♩ = 70

CHORUS

A♭maj7/B♭ A♭/B♭ E♭ Cm7

Lord, I mag - ni- fy, I glo - ri- fy, I

Fm7 B♭ A♭maj7 Fm7/A♭ Gm7

give my praise to You; Lord, I mag - ni- fy, I

Cm7 | 1. Fm7 A♭/B♭ B♭ B♭sus E♭2 A♭/B♭

glo - ri- fy, I give my praise to You. Lord, I

2. Fm7 A♭/B♭ B♭ B♭sus E♭2 Gm7

give my praise to You.

Medley options: We Worship You (FUNK); Be Magnified; We Lift You High.

For you, O Lord, are the Most High over all the earth; you are exalted far above all gods. Psalm 97:9 (NIV)

930 Lord Most High

HM-71

Words and Music by
DON HARRIS and GARY SADLER

E
Esus
E
From the hearts of the weak,
hearts of the weak,
from the
B2sus
B
from the shouts of the strong,
shouts of the strong,
from the
C♯m
from the lips of all peo - ple this
lips of all peo - ple
this
A
E/A
A
B
song we raise, Lord.
song we raise, Lord.
CHORUS
E
E/G♯
A
E/B
B7sus
E
E/G♯
Through - out the end - less ag - es You will be

Medley options: Be Exalted; May Christ Be Exalted in Me; With Our Hearts.

My soul waits for the Lord more than watchmen wait for the morning… Psalm 130:6 (NIV)

More of Your Glory

HM-73

Words and Music by
LINDELL COOLEY & BRUCE HAYNES

Medley options: Glorious God; More than Enough.

For he satisfies the thirsty and fills the hungry with good things. Psalm 107:9 (NIV)

More than Enough

HM-70

Words and Music by
DAVID BARONI and
CLAIRE CLONINGER

Am7
C/D
G
C/D
You are more than e - nough. O
You are more than e - nough. O
CHORUS
G
Gsus
G
D7sus
D7
Lord, You are more than e - nough, a
Am7
Em
Cmaj7
C/D
well - spring of mer - cy and a foun - tain of love; We
G
G/B
C
C/D
B/D♯
Em7
live to praise Your a - maz - ing grace, O Lord,
last time to Coda
A9
C/D
Em7
A9
You are more than e - nough, pre - cious Lord,

Am7
C/D
G
1.
G
2.
You are more than e-nough. 2. When we've Much
BRIDGE
F2
C2/E
more than we ask or i - mag - ine, that's
Am7(♭5)/E♭
G2/D
D/C
what Your love can do; And Lord, when Your strength fills our
Em7
Am7
G2/B
weak - ness, it's more than e - nough to
Cmaj7
C/D
D.S. al Coda
lift us to You. O

Medley options: God Is Able (ROGERS); But for Grace.

...I love you, O Lord, my strength. Psalm 18:1 (NIV)

My Jesus, I Love Thee

933

HM-69

Words and Music by
WILLIAM R. FEATHERSTONE
and ADONIRAM J. GORDON

Medley options: Fairest Lord Jesus; I Will Come and Bow Down.

I know that my Redeemer lives, and that in the end he will stand upon the earth. Job 19:25 (NIV)

934 My Redeemer Lives

HM-69

Words and Music by
EUGENE GRECO

♩ = 120

CHORUS

E/B F♯m/B E E2/G♯ A

My Re - deem - er lives, and I will see___ His glo -

A/B E/B F♯m/B E C♯m7 E2/F♯ F♯m7 A/B

ry as He works all things to - geth - er for___ my good;___

E/B F♯m/B C♯m7 Emaj7/B

___ What - ev - er things oc - cur, of

A2 E/G♯ F♯m7 A/B

this I can___ be sure,___ I know my Re -

E/B
F♯m/B
E
Fine
deem - er lives.
VERSE
G♯m7
C♯m7
E/F♯
F♯m7
E/F♯
E - ven though I walk through the val - ley,
F♯m7
A/B
B7/D♯
I will fear no e - vil, He is with
E2
Amaj7
me; And, on the bat - tle-field,
B/A
G♯m7
C♯m7
al - though the pain is real, my

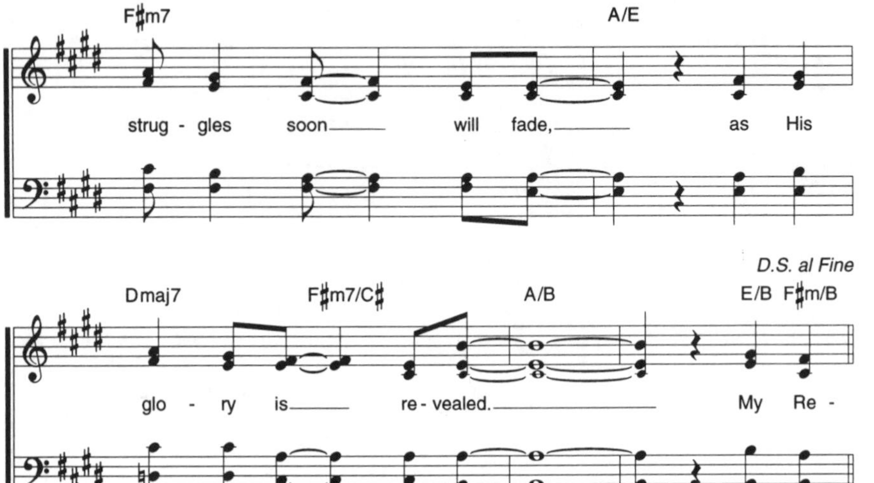

Medley options: Awesome in This Place; No Other Name; Great Is Your Name.

…His compassions never fail. They are new every morning; great is your faithfulness. Lamentations 3:22,23 (NIV)

New Every Morning

935

HM-73

Words and Music by
SCOTT UNDERWOOD

Medley options: We Praise You, Jesus; This Is the Day (SHELTON).

Behold, how good and how pleasant it is for brethren to dwell together in unity! Psalm 133:1 (KJV)

O How Good It Is

HM-72

Words and Music by
MARTIN F. BALL

Medley options: Come, Let Us Offer; We Have Come to Glorify.

May my prayer be set before you like incense; may the lifting up of my hands be like the evening sacrifice. Psalm 141:2 (NIV)

O Lord to You

937

HM-71

Words and Music by
GARY SADLER

Medley options: Highest Place; A Pure Heart.

Our help is in the name of the Lord, the Maker of heaven and earth. Psalm 124:8 (NIV)

Our Help Is in the Name

938

HM-70

Words and Music by
DAVID BARONI

Gb/Db Ebm7 Ab9 Cb/Db Cb/Gb Gb Cb/Db
1.
help is in the name of the Lord. When
VERSE
Gb Fm7(b5) Bb7(#9) Eb7sus Ebm7
troub - les seem to sur - round us, our
Gb/Ab Ab9 Abm7 Cb/Db
help is in the name of the Lord; When our
Gb Fm7(b5) Bb7(#9) Eb7sus Ebm7
en - e - mies try to con - found us, our
Gb/Ab Ab9 Cb/Db Db Bb/D
help is in the name of the Lord. God is

E♭m
E♭m/D
good, don't for - get that He's nev -
E♭m/D♭
C♭6
G♭/D♭
C♭/D♭
er failed us yet, our help, our
G♭/D♭
C♭/D♭
G♭/D♭
E♭m7
A♭9 C♭/D♭
2.
help. Our help is in the name of the Lord.
BRIDGE
C♭/G♭
G♭
B♭m7
E♭m7
His name is Je - sus, He's the
A♭m7
C♭/D♭
D♭/C♭
B♭m7
E♭m7
Rock of our sal-va - tion, Je - sus, He's the

A♭m7
C♭/D♭
D♭
B♭m7
E♭m7
lift - er of our heads; His name is Je - sus, our
A♭m7
C♭/D♭
D♭/C♭
B♭m7
E♭m7
hope in trib - u - la - tion, His name is Je - sus, the
A♭m7
C♭/D♭
D♭
B m7
E m7
on - ly One we turn to. Je - sus, He's the
A m7
C/D
D/C
B m7
E m7
Rock of our sal - va - tion, Je - sus, He's the
A m7
C/D
D/C
B m7
E m7
lift - er of our heads; His name is Je - sus, our

A m7
C/D
D
hope in trib - u - la - tion, Prince
G
D/F♯
G/F
C/E
of Peace, Lord and King, Might - y God is He, our
G/D
C/D
G/D
C/D
help our help our
G/D
E m7
A 9
C/D
help is in the name of the Lord. Our
CHORUS
G
C/G
G 9
help is in the name of the Lord, our

Medley options: God Gives His children a Song; Send It on Down.

…May all who seek You rejoice and be glad in You; may those who love your salvation always say, "the Lord be exalted!" Psalm 40:16 (NIV)

People Just Like Us

HM-68

Words and Music by
RUSSELL FRAGAR

B+
Em
(echo)
Makes you wan - na dance, makes you wan - na dance,
Cmaj7
(echo)
makes you wan - na sing, makes you wan - na sing;
Am7
Makes you wan - na shout all a - bout it, shout
Bm
B+
all a - bout it, shout it that Je - sus is King.
VERSE
Em
D
Ev-'ry na-tion, pow'r, and tongue will bow down to Your name,

F
ev - 'ry eye will see, ev - 'ry ear will
Em
C D Em
hear Your name pro - claimed; This is gon - na be
D
F
our cry un - til You come a - gain, "Je - sus is the on -
Cmaj7
D
ly name by which man can be saved." All o - ver the
CHORUS
G
Am
world, peo - ple just like us are call - ing Your name,

Em F G
— liv-ing in Your love; — All — o - ver the world, — peo- ple just like us —
Am Cmaj7 Bm7 Cmaj7 Bm7 C/D
— are fol-low-ing Je - sus. — All — o - ver the
G Am
world, peo - ple just like us — are call - ing Your name, —
Em F G
— liv-ing in Your love; — All — o - ver the world, — peo- ple just like us —
Am Cmaj7 Bm7 Cmaj7 Bm7 Cmaj7 Bm7
1.
— are fol-low-ing Je - sus. —

Medley options: Sing to the Lord All the Earth (CHRISTENSEN);
Mighty Is Our God.

...and have put on the new self, which is being renewed in knowledge in the image of the Creator. Colossians 3:10 (NIV)

940 Power of Your Love

HM-68

Words and Music by
GEOFF BULLOCK

D♭ E♭ D♭/E♭ D♭/A♭ A♭ E♭/G Fm7 E♭
way by the pow'r of Your love.
day by the pow'r of Your love.
CHORUS
D♭ Fm E♭ D♭/A♭ A♭ E♭/G Fm7 E♭
Hold me close, let Your love sur - round me,
D♭ Fm E♭ A♭ B♭m7
bring me near, draw me to Your side;
A♭/C E♭m7 A♭ D♭ Fm E♭ D♭/A♭
And as I wait I'll rise up like the ea -
A♭ E♭/G Fm E♭
gle, and I will soar with You, Your Spir - it leads me

Medley options: Your Great Love (CHRISTENSEN); Lord, I Thirst for You.

Praise the Lord, all you nations, extol him, all you peoples. Psalm 117:1 (NIV)

Praise the Lord All Nations

941

Words and Music by
PAUL BALOCHE
and ED KERR

W. L.
Ju - bi-lee!
Cong.
Ju - bi-lee!
W. L.
You know the
time for ju - bi-lee is here,
Cong.
the time for ju - bi-lee is here;
W. L.
The
time for ju - bi-lee is here,
Cong.
the time for ju - bi-lee is here.

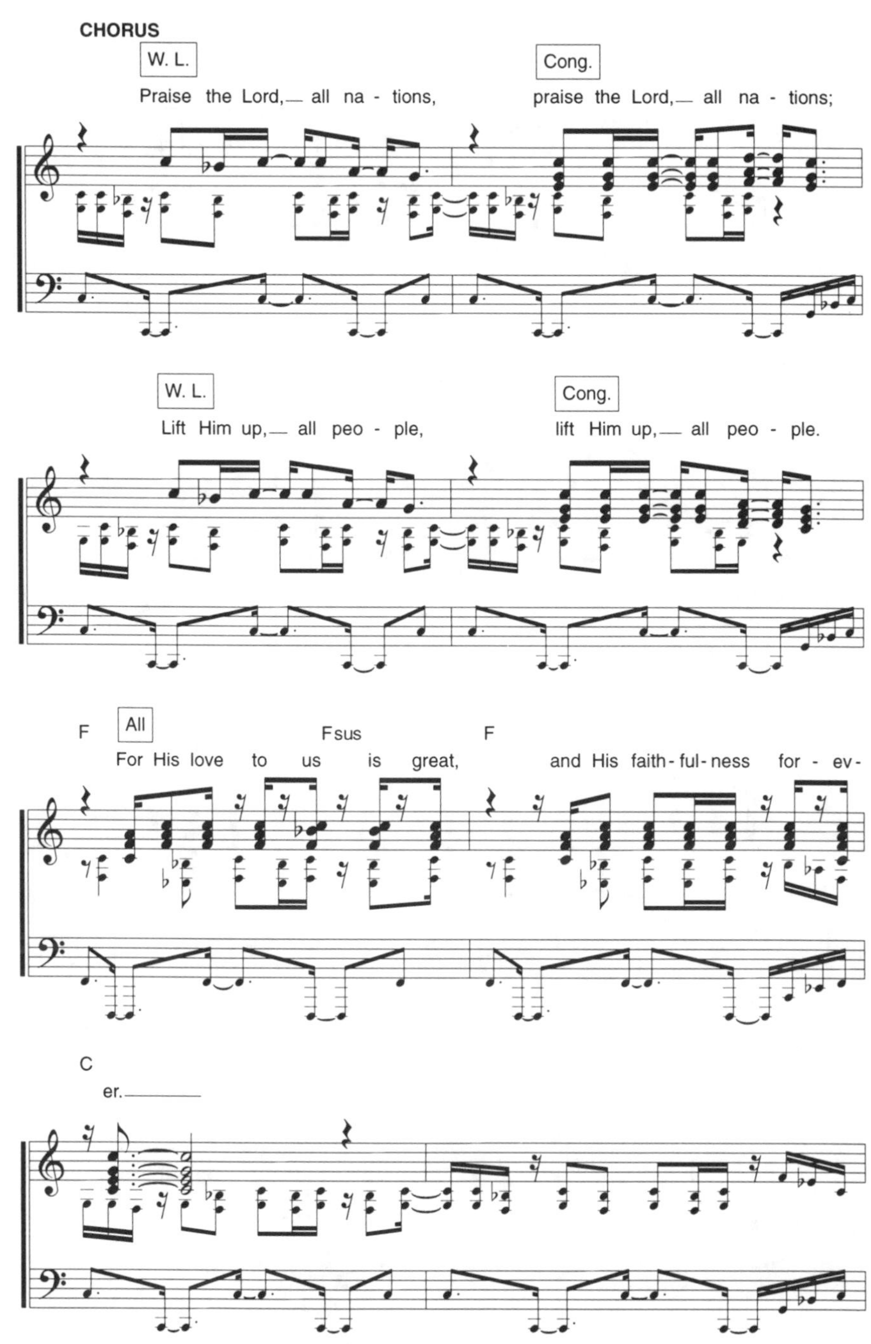

CHORUS
W. L.
Praise the Lord, all na - tions,
Cong.
praise the Lord, all na - tions;
W. L.
Lift Him up, all peo - ple,
Cong.
lift Him up, all peo - ple.
F
All
For His love to us is great,
Fsus
F
and His faith - ful - ness for - ev -
C
er.

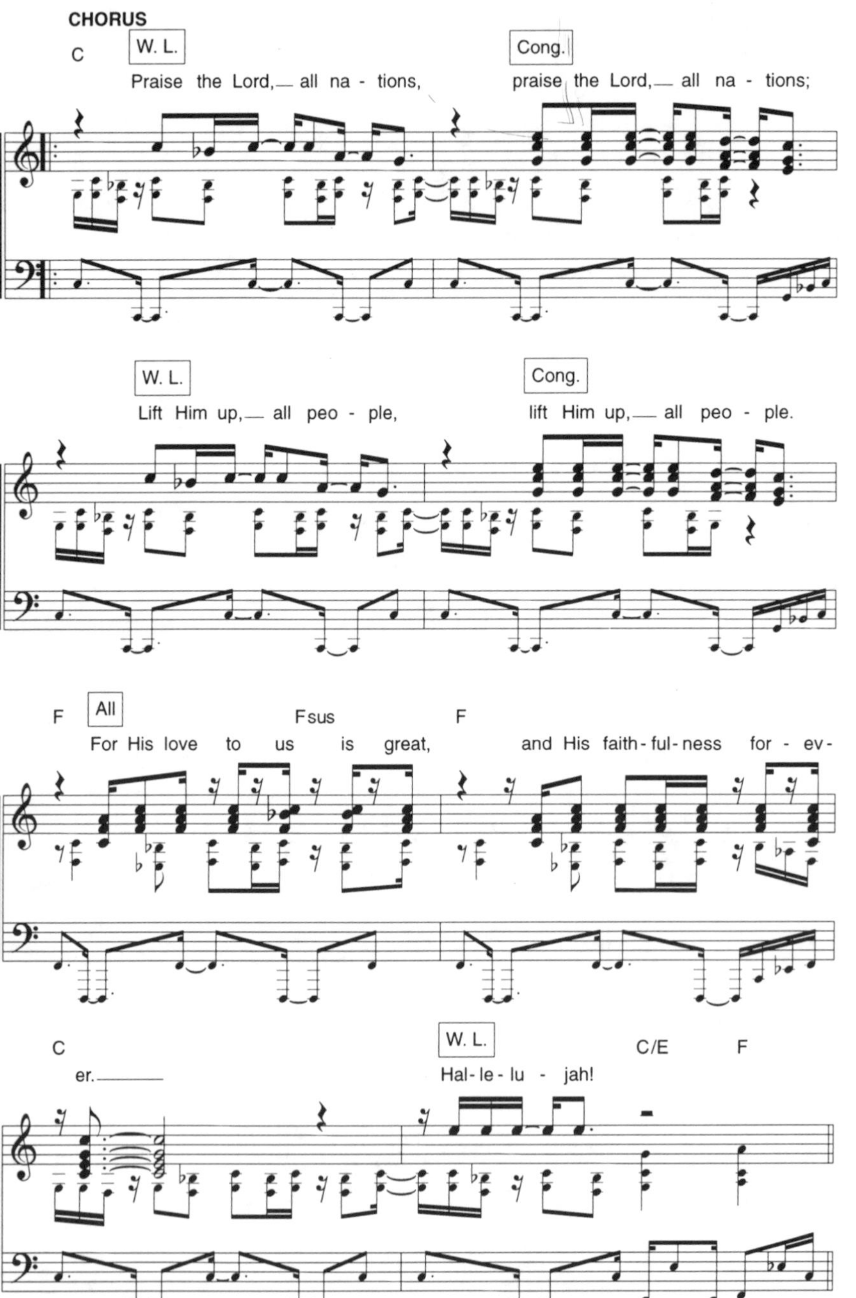
CHORUS
C
W. L.
Praise the Lord, all na - tions,
Cong.
praise the Lord, all na - tions;
W. L.
Lift Him up, all peo - ple,
Cong.
lift Him up, all peo - ple.
F
All
For His love to us is great,
Fsus
F
and His faith-ful-ness for - ev -
C
er.
W. L.
Hal-le-lu - jah!
C/E
F

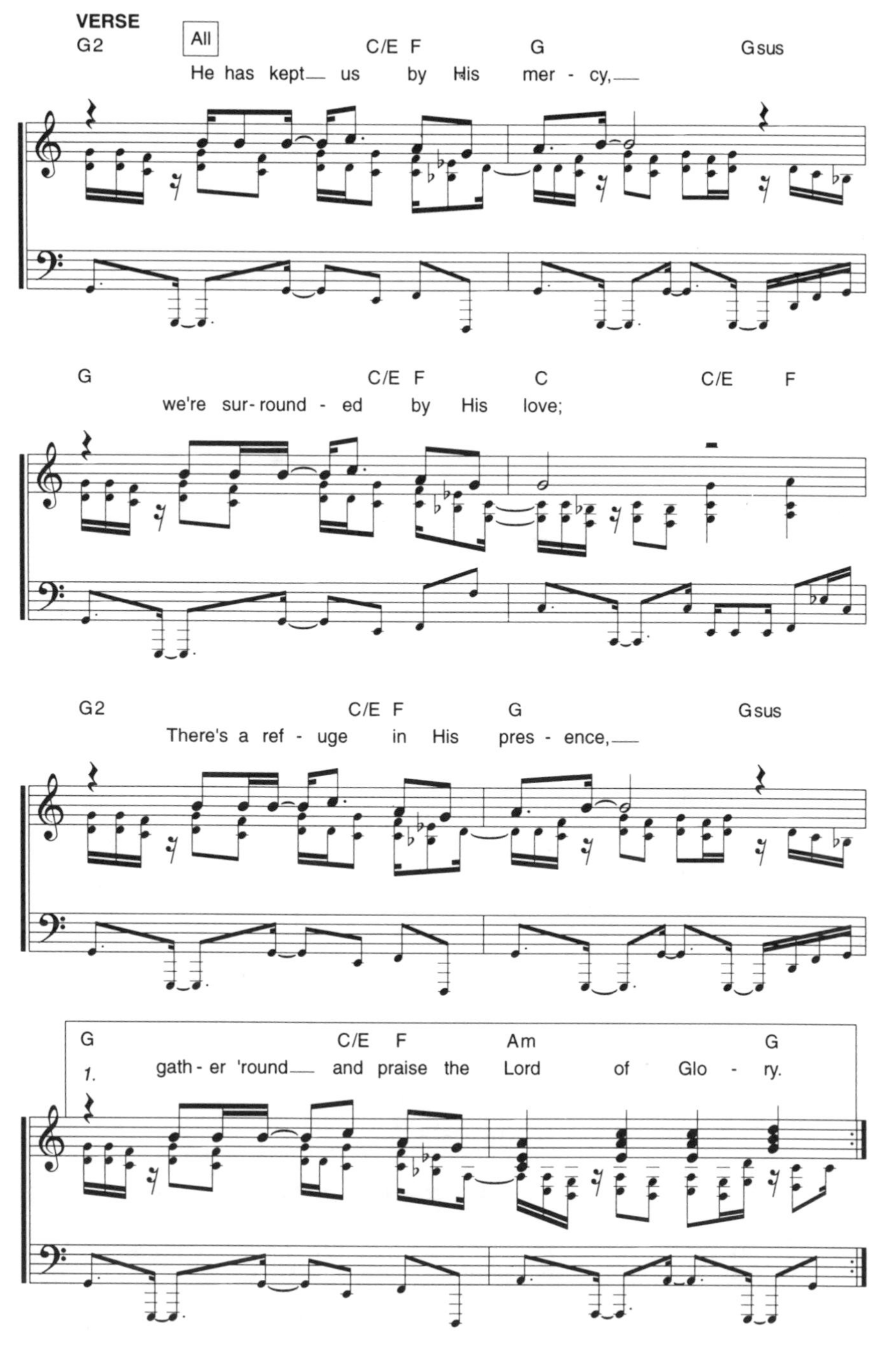

VERSE
G2
All
C/E F
G
Gsus
He has kept us by His mer - cy,
G
C/E F
C
C/E
F
we're sur-round - ed by His love;
G2
C/E F
G
Gsus
There's a ref - uge in His pres - ence,
G
C/E F
Am
G
1. gath - er 'round and praise the Lord of Glo - ry.

G
C/E F
Am
Women
2. gath- er 'round and praise the Lord. Praise the Lord,
TAG
B♭2
F2
Lord of glo - ry, praise the Lord!
Men
Praise the Lord,
Lord of glo - ry, praise the Lord!
C
Praise the Lord,
B♭2
F2
repeat 3 times
Lord of glo - ry, praise the Lord!
Praise the Lord,
Lord of glo - ry, praise the Lord!

Medley options: Shout It Loud; Resound in Praise.

Sing to God, O kingdoms of the earth, sing praise to the Lord. Psalm 68:32 (NIV)

942 Praise to the Lord

HM-71

Words and Music by
BOB FITTS

Medley options: Praise to You; I Exalt Thee; Lord, We Welcome You.

Rejoice in the Lord and be glad, you righteous… Psalm 32:11 (NIV)

943

Rejoice

HM-69

Words and Music by
PAUL BALOCHE
and DON HARRIS

Csus C Gm11 F C Dm
Sing hal - le -
and shout for joy;
Sing hal - le -
Re - joice in the Lord, sing hal - le -
B♭ F/A Gm7 F/A B♭ Csus C
lu - jah!
D
1.
lu jah, hal - le - lu. Re - joice!
lu - jah.
G2 A7sus
3
You give
VERSE
D A G2
beau - ty for ash - es, com - fort for pain,
D Bm7 G A G2/B
laugh - ter for sad - ness in Your name;

Medley options: Always (BALOCHE); I Love to Be in Your Presence; We Rejoice.

Lord, I have heard of your fame; I stand in awe of your deeds, O Lord. Renew them in our day… Habakkuk 3:2 (NIV)

Renew Them in Our Day

HM-72

Words and Music by
MARTIN F. BALL and
MIKE GODWARD

Medley options: Be Exalted, O God; Shout to the Lord.

…My soul finds rest in God alone… Psalm 62:1 (NIV)

Rest in Your Love

945

HM-69

Words and Music by
GARY SADLER

Cm7
Fm11
ence, I will rest, I will rest
A♭/B♭
B♭
E♭
A♭/E♭
E♭2
Fine
in Your love.
VERSE
A♭maj7
B♭sus
B♭
G7(♭9)/B
1. Whom shall I fear, why should I wor -
2. All of my doubts, all of my striv -
Cm
Fm7
A♭/B♭
ry? Your grace is e - nough for my need.
ing, by faith I lay down at Your throne;
E♭2
E♭2/G
A♭
B♭/A♭
Your joy is my strength, Your
Your Word is my shield, Your

Medley options: Your Steadfast Love; I Look to You.

…One more powerful than I will come… He will baptize you with the Holy Spirit and with fire. Luke 3:16 (NIV)

946 Revival Fire, Fall

Words and Music by
PAUL BALOCHE

HM-73

ALL
D/F♯ Em7
Pour out from Heav - en Your pas - sion and pres - ence,
A D/A A
bring down Your burn - ing de - sire. Re -
CHORUS
D D/F♯ G Em7 Asus A7 D D/F♯ G Em7 Asus A7
viv - al fire, fall, re - viv - al fire, fall;
Bm F♯m7
Fall on us here in the pow'r of Your Spir - it,
G D/A A7 D D/F♯ G Em7
Fa - ther, let re - viv - al fire fall. Re - viv - al fire,

Medley options: No Eye Has Seen (CHISUM/TAYLOR); Heaven and Earth.

Praise be to the God and Father of our Lord Jesus Christ,
the Father of compassion and the God of all comfort… 2 Corinthians 1:3 (NIV)

947

Shout to the Lord

HM-68

Words and Music by
DARLENE ZSCHECH

♩ = 76

VERSE

A E F♯m E
My Je-sus, my Sav-ior, Lord, there is none like You;

D A/C♯ D A/E F♯m
All of my days I want to praise the won-ders of Your

G D/F♯ Esus E D/E A E
might-y love. My com-fort, my Shel-ter,

F♯m E D
Tow-er of ref-uge and strength; Let ev-'ry breath,

A/C♯ D A/E F♯m G D/F♯ Esus E
all that I am, never cease to worship You.
CHORUS
A F♯m D D/E E
Shout to the Lord, all the earth, let us sing
A F♯m D Esus E
power and majesty, praise to the King;
F♯m D
Mountains bow down and the seas will roar at the
E F♯m E/G♯ A F♯m
sound of Your name. I sing for joy at the work

Medley options: Shout It Loud; We Declare Your Name; All Hail King Jesus.

Shouts of joy and victory resound in the tents of the righteous… Psalm 118:15 (NIV)

948

Shouts of Joy

HM-70

Words and Music by
PAUL BALOCHE
and ED KERR

D E/D G/A
Join in the time-less cel - e-bra - tion,
Bm7 E7 G/A
of - fer your heart to Him a-lone;
D E/D C♯m7 F♯m7 E/F♯
Wor-ship His ev - er-last-ing maj - es - ty,
Bm7 D/E E G/A
with an-gels and saints a-round the throne.
CHORUS
D Em7 D/F♯ C/G G C/G G Am/G G
Praise the Lord with sing - ing,

Medley options: Resound in Praise; Ancient of Days.

...Let the wise listen and add to their learning, and let the discerning get guidance... Proverbs 1:5 (NIV)

Show Me Your Ways

HM-68

Words and Music by
RUSSELL FRAGAR

♪ = 116

G/A D Em/D D Bm7 Em/B

Show me Your ways that I may walk with

Bm7 G D Em/D D Bm7 Em/B

You, show me Your ways, I put my hope in

Bm7 F♯m/A G D/F♯ Em7

You; The cry of my heart is to love You more, to

A A/G F♯m7

live with the touch of Your hand, strong - er each

Medley options: Blessing, Glory, and Honor (SULANDER);
I will Bless the Lord (HERNANDEZ).

The Lord reigns, let the earth be glad; let the distant shores rejoice. Psalm 97:1 (NIV)

Sing Hallelujah

HM-71

Words and Music by
BOB FITTS

Medley options: God Is Able (FITTS); We Rejoice.

The Spirit of the Sovereign Lord is on me, because the Lord has anointed me
to preach good news to the poor… Isaiah 61:1 (NIV)

Spirit of the Sovereign God

951

Words and Music by
ANDY PARK

HM-73

Gm F/G Gm
cause He has a-noint - ed you to preach good
cause He has a-noint - ed us to preach good
Worship Leader
F E♭ Cm
1. He has sent you to the poor
2. He will com - fort all who mourn,
news.
news.
F B♭/F F B♭/D E♭ Cm
to bind up the bro - ken - heart -
He will pro - vide for those who grieve
This is the year,
This is the year,
F B♭/F F B♭/D E♭ Cm
ed;
To bring free-dom to the cap -
in Zi - on;
He's pour - ing out His oil of glad -
this is the day,
this is the day,

F Bb/F F Bb/D Eb Cm
tives and to re-lease the ones in
ness, in-stead of mourn-ing we will
this is the year.
this is the year.
CHORUS
Fsus F Bb Bb/D Eb Eb/G
dark - ness.
praise.
This is the year,
F Bb F/A Gm Eb
Of the fa - vor of the Lord,
this is the day;
F Bb F/A Gm Eb
of the venge-ance of our God;
This is the year,

Medley options: Send Your Rain; Awesome God.

For it is by grace you have been saved, through faith… Ephesians 2:8 (NIV)

Standing by Your Grace

952

HM-72

Words and Music by
MARTIN F. BALL
and RACHEL BALL

Gm F C2 Gm F
sin and though dis - grace tried to keep us from this
want to see Your face and know Your warm em -
see the love You gave, dai - ly in our lives dis -
C2 E♭ F Gm
place, the pre - cious blood You gave re -
brace, we've come to wait on You, Lord
played, may all we say and do bring
Cm
1.
Dsus D Gm F B♭maj7/D
moved our guilt and shame.
show us what to
glo - ry un - to
C2 E♭2 F2 Dsus/G

CHORUS
Dsus D G G/B C C/D
2,3.
do.
You.
We a-dore You, Lord,
G G/B C Cm6 G/B
we ex-alt Your name, for You're mag-nif-i-cent,
Am Am/G D/F♯ C6/E D C/D G G/B
wor-thy of praise; All glo-ry be to
C C/D G G/B C Cm6
You, for there is none like You, Je-sus, You're
G/B G Am7 G/B C Cm6 G/B G Am7 G/B
won-der-ful, Lord, You are mag-nif-i-cent,

Medley options: Jesus, We Enthrone You; Crown Him King of Kings.

Surely goodness and mercy shall follow me all the days of my life… Psalm 23:6 (NKJ)

Surely Goodness and Mercy 953

HM-69

Words and Music by
CARL ALBRECHT, JAMIE HARVILL
and MARTIN J. NYSTROM

Medley options: Celebrate the Lord of Love; Mourning Into Dancing; God Is Good All the Time.

I saw the Holy City, the new Jerusalem, coming down out of heaven from God… Revelation 21:2 (NIV)

Sweepin' Through the City 954

HM-74

Author unknown

C♭/E♭
N. C.
A♭
1.
won't, I won't be back, I won't be back, I won't be back no
C♭/D♭ D♭/E♭ D♭/G♭ A♭ E♭7(♯9)
more, no more, no more. We'll go
C♭/E♭
N. C.
A♭
2.
won't, I won't be back, I won't be back, I won't be back no
C♭/D♭ D♭/E♭ D♭/G♭ A♭ E♭7(♯9)
more, no more, no more.
VERSE
A♭9 D♭/A♭ A♭9 D♭/A♭
Bless - ed are the pure in heart, for

A♭9 D♭/A♭ C♭/D♭ D♭/E♭
they'll go sweep - in' through the cit - y;
A♭9 D♭/A♭ A♭9 D♭/A♭
Bless - ed are those that mourn, for
A♭9 D♭/A♭ C♭/D♭ D♭/E♭
they'll go sweep - in' through the cit - y.
A♭9 D♭/A♭ A♭9 D♭/A♭
Bless - ed are the poor in spir - it, for
A♭9 D♭/A♭ C♭/D♭ D♭/E♭
they'll go sweep - in' through the cit - y;

A♭9
D♭/A♭
A♭9
Bless - ed are the peace - mak - ers,
A♭
E♭7(+5,♯9)
for they'll go
C♭/E♭
N. C.
3.
won't, I won't be back, I won't be back, I won't be back,
C♭/E♭
I won't be back, I won't be back, I won't be back,
C♭/E♭
A♭
I won't be back, I won't be back, I won't be back no

Medley option: When We All Get to Heaven.

...Give thanks to the Lord, for he is good... Psalm 106:1 (NIV)

955 Take a Little Time

HM-73

Words and Music by
ANDRAE CROUCH

Medley options: I Need You More; I Love to Love You.

The Lord said to him, "What is that in your hand?"... Exodus 4:2 (NIV)

956 That's When (He Steps In)

HM-70

Words and Music by
HELENA BARRINGTON

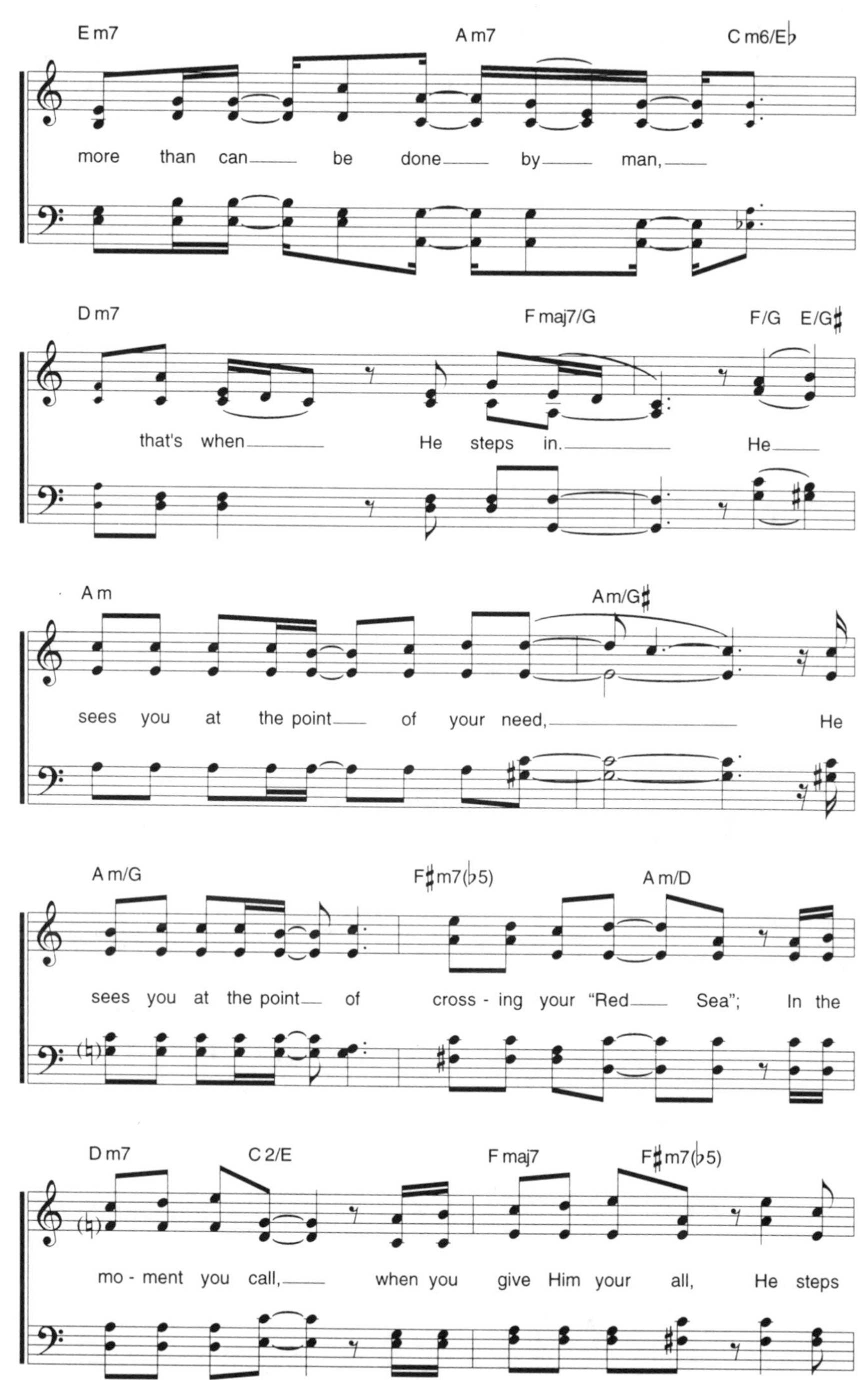
Em7
Am7
Cm6/E♭
more than can__ be done__ by__ man,__
Dm7
Fmaj7/G
F/G E/G♯
that's when__ He steps in.__ He__
Am
Am/G♯
sees you at the point__ of your need,__ He
Am/G
F♯m7(♭5)
Am/D
sees you at the point__ of cross - ing your "Red__ Sea"; In the
Dm7
C2/E
Fmaj7
F♯m7(♭5)
mo - ment you call,__ when you give Him your all, He steps

Dm7 Fmaj7/G F/G G7(♭9)
in, He steps in. And He'll say,
CHORUS
C Em7 Am7 Dm7
"what's that you have in your hand? I can use it, if you're
Fmaj7/G F/G G C Em7 Am7
will - ing to lose it; Take the lit - tle you have and make it grand,
Dm7 Fmaj7/G G7
I am El Shad - dai, and I'll more than sup - ply your
C A♭maj7 Fmaj7/G
1.
need." When

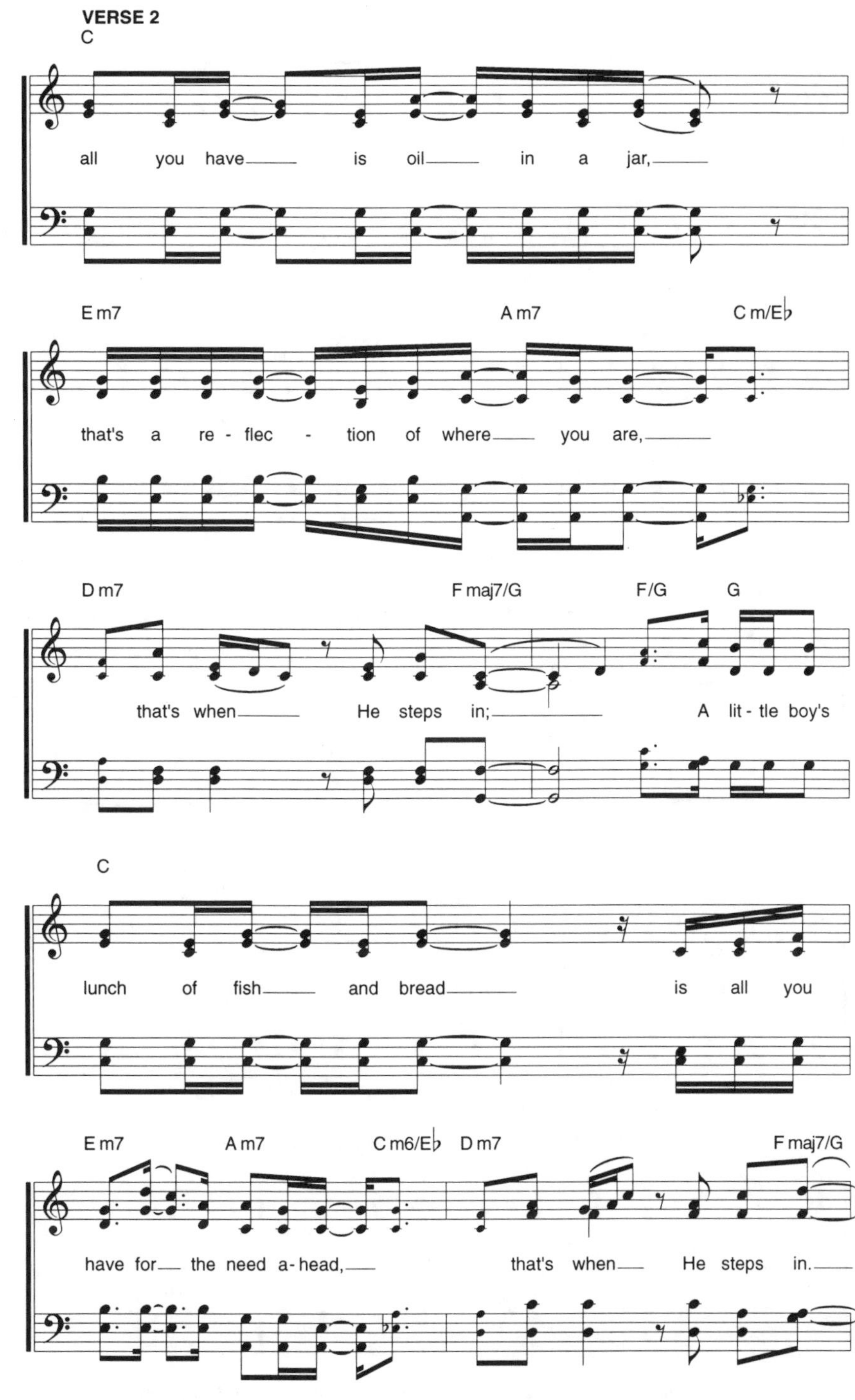
VERSE 2
C
all you have is oil in a jar,
Em7
Am7
Cm/E♭
that's a re - flec - tion of where you are,
Dm7
Fmaj7/G
F/G
G
that's when He steps in; A lit - tle boy's
C
lunch of fish and bread is all you
Em7
Am7
Cm6/E♭
Dm7
Fmaj7/G
have for the need a - head, that's when He steps in.

Medley options: No Eye Has Seen (BALOCHE/KERR); Bread to the Nations.

The Lord reigns, let the earth be glad… Psalm 97:1 (NIV)

The Lord Reigns

957

HM-73

Words and Music by
DAN STRADWICK

Medley options: All the Earth; Jesus Shall Reign.

There is a river whose streams make glad the city of God… Psalm 46:4 (NIV)

The River Is Here

958

HM-71

Words and Music by
ANDY PARK

VERSE

♩ = 117

B♭ F C F

1. Down the moun - tain, the riv - er flows, and it
2. The riv - er of God is teem - ing with life, and
3. Up to the moun - tain we love to go, to

B♭ F C F

brings re - fresh - ing wher - ev - er it goes;
all who touch it can be re - vived; And
find the pres - ence of the Lord; A -

B♭ F C F

Through the val - leys and o - ver the fields, the
all who lin - ger on this riv - er's shore will
long the banks of the riv - er we run, we

B♭ F C F

riv - er is rush - ing, and the riv - er is here. The
come back thirst - ing for more of the Lord. The
dance with laugh - ter, giv - ing praise to the Son. The

Medley options: Celebrate the Lord of Love; Firm Foundation.

I have sought your face with all my heart... Psalm 119:58 (NIV)

The Shadow of Your Face

959

HM-71

Words and Music by
BOB FITTS

G D A
breathe with-out Your breath; I can-not sing with-out Your song,
D G D G
O Lord, ring-ing deep-ly in my breast.
CHORUS
Em7 A D G
Where can I go from Your pres-ence, Lord? You are
Em7 A D Em7 A D
with me all of my days; In my deep-est de-spair to the high-
D/F♯ G D/F♯
est place, I will re-main

Medley options: Sanctify My Heart; For the Lord Is Good.

How great are his signs, how mighty his wonders!... Daniel 4:3 (NIV)

960 The Wonders of His Hands

HM-70

Words and Music by
GERON DAVIS

CHORUS
Em Bm Am7 C/D
mazed when I see all He's done, and to think He did it
D/G G Bm7 Em Bm Em
all for me; O, how great, O, how grand are the
Am7 C/D G C/G
great and might - y won - ders of His hands.
D/G C/G C D
On a
VERSE 2
Bm Em Am E2 sus Em
hill, on a cross, He stretched

D6 Am7 Bm7
out His hands___ to save___ a world___ so
Cmaj7 Bm Am Dsus D/C Bm Em
lost;___ But in the pain___ was a
Am7 Gmaj7/B C Am7 C/D
plan, this would be___ the great - est won - der of His
VERSE 3
G2 D♭/E♭ A♭ Fm7 B♭m7 D♭ D♭/F
hands. Bro - ken hearts,___ torn by sin, with one
E♭/G G♭° D♭2/F B♭m7(♭5)/F♭ A♭/E♭ Dm7(♭5) D♭maj7 D♭/E♭
touch of His hand___ new a - gain;___ Born in love,_

A♭ Cm Fm B♭m7 A♭/C D♭ B♭m7
free to stand as a glo-
D♭/E♭ A♭ Cm
rious new cre-a-tion of His hands. And I'm a-
CHORUS
Fm Cm Fm B♭m7 D♭/E♭
mazed when I see all He's done, and to know He did it
E♭/A♭ A♭ Cm7 Fm Cm Fm
all for me; O, how great to know I am stand-ing
B♭m7 D♭/E♭ A♭ Cm Fm
here as a won-der of His hands. Un-a-shamed I will

Medley options: Mercy Saw Me; In Your Presence, O God.

This is the day the Lord has made; let us rejoice and be glad in it. Psalm 118:24 (NIV)

This Is the Day

961

HM-71

Words and Music by
BOB FITTS

♩ = 132

CHORUS

F

This is the day that the Lord has made,

Csus C Csus

I will rejoice and celebrate;

C B♭ C F

This is the day that the Lord has made,

B♭ F/A B♭ F/C B♭/C

I will rejoice, I will rejoice and celebrate.

F
Bb C F
Bb/C
1.
F
Bb C F
Bb
2.
He goes be-fore

VERSE

F
Bb/F
F
Bb
F
Bb/F
He goes be-fore me,
He walks be-side
me,
He walks be-side me,

F
Bb
F
Dm7
Gm7
F/C
me, He lives with-in me, He's the Lov-er of my soul;

C Csus
C Bb/C
F
Bb/F
He's my de-fend-
He's my de-fend - er,

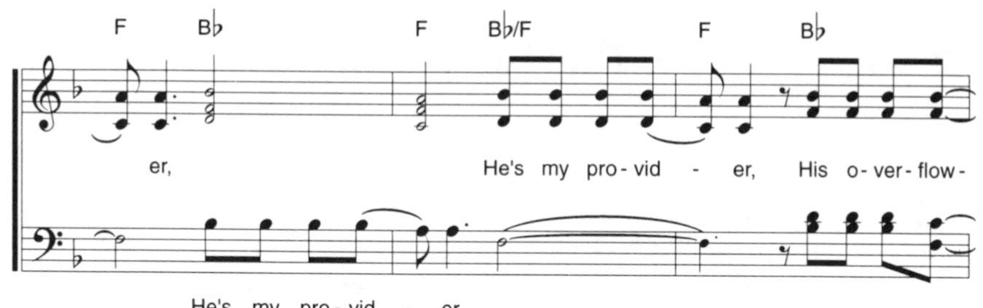

Medley options: I Love to Be in Your Presence; Glory, Glory, Lord.

For the kingdom of God is not a matter of talk but of power. 1 Corinthians 4:20 (NIV)

962 This Kingdom

HM-68

Words and Music by
GEOFF BULLOCK

G Em7 A G/A F♯m/A Em7/A
fied, His king - dom comes. And this
fied, His king - dom comes. And this
CHORUS
D A/C♯ Bm
king- dom will know no end, and it s glo- ry shall know no bounds,
F♯m/A G A/G D/F♯
for the maj- es - ty and pow - er of this
E/G♯ Asus A Bm A/C♯
king - dom's King has come; And this
D A/C♯
king - dom's reign, and this king - dom's rule, and this

Medley options: I Exalt Thee; We Will Glorify; You Are Glorious.

"Be still, and know that I am God; I will be exalted among the nations, I will be exalted in the earth." Psalm 46:10 (NIV)

We Are Stilled

963

HM-72

Words and Music by
MARTIN F. BALL and
IAN THOMPSON

Medley options: Our Heart; In the Presence.

…"In the time of my favor I heard you, and in the day of salvation I helped you." 2 Corinthians 6:2 (NIV)

We Have Called on You, Lord 964

HM-72

Words and Music by
STUART DAVID GARRARD

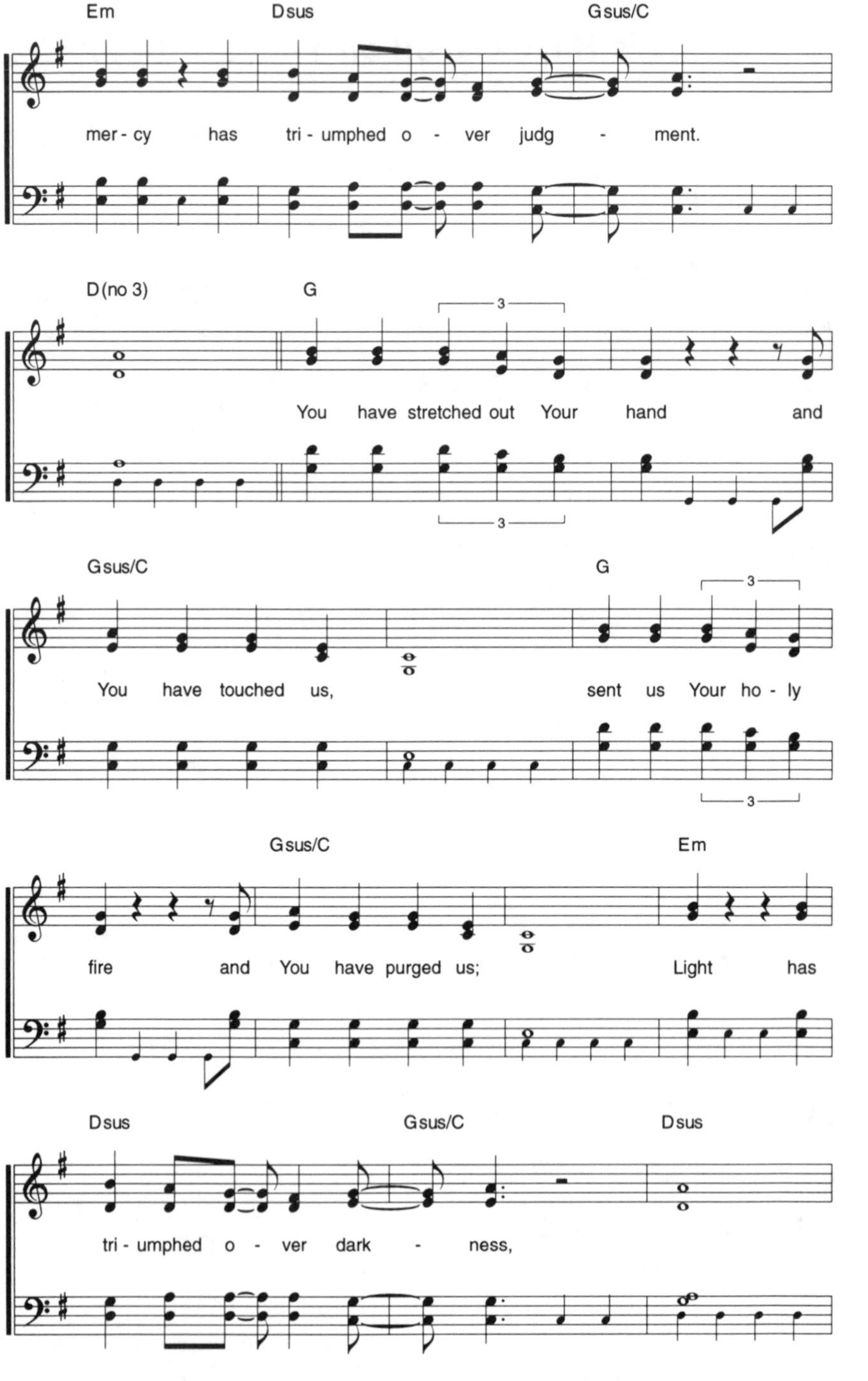

Em Dsus Gsus/C
mer - cy has tri - umphed o - ver judg - ment.
D(no 3) G
You have stretched out Your hand and
Gsus/C G
You have touched us, sent us Your ho - ly
Gsus/C Em
fire and You have purged us; Light has
Dsus Gsus/C Dsus
tri - umphed o - ver dark - ness,

Em
Dsus
light has tri - umphed o - ver dark -
Gsus/C
D(no 3)
ness. We love
CHORUS
G
G/F
C/E
You and sing to You, God of our sal - va -
D
G
G/F
tion; You've res - cued us and we de - clare Your
C/E
G/D
D
Em
C
glo - ry to the na - tions. We give our lives,

G
Dsus
D
Em
a liv - ing sac - ri - fice;
Emp - ty and
C
Dsus
D
3rd time to Coda
read - y to be filled
with Your
3
3
G
Gsus/C
G
1.
pow - er.
Gsus/C
D7sus
G
2.
pow - er.
Gsus/C
Em
D
D.S. al Coda
We love

Medley options: Great Is the Lord (CHRISTENSEN); Sing to the Lord All the Earth.

…When he appears, we shall be like him, for we shall see him as he is. 1 John 3:2 (NIV)

965 We Shall See the King

Medley option: We Will Ride.

Let us draw near to God with a sincere heart… Hebrews 10:22 (NIV)

966 We Will Draw Near

HM-69

Words and Music by
MARTIN J. NYSTROM
and DON HARRIS

D7sus
1.
D
G
C/G
G
You will draw near to us. We want to be like
VERSE
D/C
C
D
G
D/F♯
Ma - ry, who found the bet - ter part;
Em7
G/D
C
D
C/E
D/F♯
We want to be like John, who laid his head up - on Your
G
Am7
C/D
D/C
Bm7
heart. We are not con - tent to wor - ship from a - far;
Em7
D/E
Em7
Am
Cmaj7/G
D/F♯
D
C/D
Draw us near to Your heart, O God.

Medley options: I Sing Praises; I Want to Be Where You Are.

The armies of heaven were following him, riding on white horses
and dressed in fine linen, white and clean. Revelation 19:14 (NIV)

967

We Will Ride

HM-73

Words and Music by
ANDY PARK

Gsus/C
sword in His hand, He's rid - ing a white horse all a -
G
C/G
cross this land. He's call - ing out to you and me,
G7
C
F/C
C
"will you ride with me"? He has
C
Dm/C
C
fire in His eyes and a sword in His hand, and He's
Ooo

C Dm/C C C/E
rid - ing a white horse a - cross this land; He's
Ooo Ooo
F
call - ing out to you and me, "will you ride with
Ah
C Dm/C C G
me, will you ride with me"? We say, "yes,
Ooo Yes, Lord,
C Dm/C C C Dm/C
we'll ride with You." And we say, "yes, Lord
Yes, Lord,

C
C
Dm/C
C
F
we will stand up and fight; We will ride
we will stand up and fight; We will ride,
with the ar-mies of Heav-en," gon-na be dressed in white
C
G
We say, "yes, Lord,
we'll be dressed in white.
Yes, Lord,
C
Dm/C
C
we'll ride with You."
He has a

C
Dm/C
C
crown on His head, He car - ries a scep - ter in His hand;
Ooo
C
Dm/C
C
C/E
He's lead-ing the ar - mies all a - cross this land.
And He's
Ooo
Ooo
F
call - ing out to you and me,
"will you ride
Ah
C
Dm/C
C
with me,
will you ride
with me"?
We say,
Ooo

G
C
"yes, Lord,
we will ride.
And we say,
Yes, Lord,
ride.
C
Dm/C
C
"yes, Lord,
gon - na stand up and fight;
Yes, Lord,
Dm/C
C
F
We will ride
we will stand up and fight;
We will ride
with the ar - mies of Heav - en."
We're gon - na be dressed in white.

C
3
G
Can I hear you say, "yes, Lord,
we'll be dressed in white.
Yes, Lord,
C
C
Dm/C
we will ride."
We say,
"yes, Lord,
ride.
Yes, Lord,
C
Dm/C
C
F
gon-na stand up.
we will stand up and fight;
We will ride,
3
We're gon-na ride with the ar-mies of Heav-en, gon-na be dressed in white.

C
If I were you, I would say,
we'll be dressed in white.
G
C Dm/C C
"yes, Lord, we will ride."
Yes, Lord,
Dm/C C
C
Dm/C
That fire in His eyes is His
Ooo
C
Dm/C
C
Dm/C
love for His Bride, and He's long - ing that she be with Him,
Ooo

C
C/E
F
3
right by His side;
Yes, that fire in His eyes is His
Ooo
Ah
C
Dm/C
burn-ing de-sire
that His Bride be with Him,
right by His
Ooo
C
G
side;
Can you hear Him
call-ing out
to us right now,
G7
C Dm/C C Dm/C C
Dm/C C
"will you ride with me"?
Yes, Lord,
yes, Lord.
Yes, Lord,
yes, Lord.

Medley options: Lord, I'm Gonna Love You; We Shall See the King.

...His father saw him...he ran to his son, threw his arms around him and kissed him. Luke 15:20 (NIV)

Welcome Home

968

HM-74

Words and Music by
RON KENOLY

Fm7
Ab/Bb
Bb/Ab
a - wait - ing my re - turn;
3
Gm11
Cm
Bb/C
Cm
A7(b5)
Near them stood my fa- ther with his arms stretched out to me, with
Ab2
Eb2/G
Fm7
Ab/Bb
3
tears on his face I heard him say, "wel - come
Gm7
Bb/C
Gsus/E
home. I've missed you so much, my

Fm7
B♭/C
Cm
3
heart has been bro - ken since the
E♭/A♭
A♭
A♭/B♭
G♭M9♯5/A♭
Gm7
3
day you went a-way; Wel-come home, I'll pre -
B♭/C
C9(♭5)
C9
pare a cel - e - bra - tion, come,
A♭2
A♭
E♭2/G
E♭/G
3
Fm7
take your place be-side me, you've been gone so long,

A♭/B♭
A♭/E♭
E♭2/G
Fm7
A♭/B♭
wel- come home."
E♭maj7
His hand was on my shoul - der
Fm7
E♭2/G
as we walked up to the house,
A♭2
A♭
E♭2/G
E♭/G
and Mom peeped out the front door

Fm7
Ab/Bb
Bb/Ab
and then came run - ning out; She
Gm11
threw her arms a - round me and
Cm
Bb/C
Cm
A7(b5)
squeezed me like on - ly Mom - ma can, and then
Ab2
Eb2/G
kissed me on my cheek and with my

Fm7
A♭/B♭
Gm7
face held in her hands she said, "wel- come home. How I've
B♭/C
Gsus/E
Fm7
B♭/C Cm
longed for this mo- ment, I've prayed for you each night since the
E♭/A♭
A♭
A♭/B♭
G♭M9♯5/A♭
Gm7
3
day you went a- way; Wel - come home, I'll pre-
B♭/C
C9(♭5)
C9
pare a place for you, my

A♭2 A♭ E♭2/G E♭/G
prayers have been an - swered, thank You,
Fm7 A♭/B♭
Je - sus, O, thank You, Je - sus, wel - come
A♭/E♭ E♭ F/A G/B Cm Cm2/B
home." O, how good it felt to
Cm/B♭ A♭ E♭/G
be in my fa - ther's house, af - ter

Fm7
D♭maj9
all the pain and heart - ache I had
E♭maj7
G7♯5
put him through; And to
Cm
Cm2/B
Cm/B♭
A♭
E♭/G
know that I'm for - giv - en and my past has been for - got - ten, and to
Fm7
A♭/B♭
Gm7
B♭/C
C2/B♭
hear my fam-'ly say, "we still love you." O,

Am7
C/D
C/E D/F♯
welcome home, O how sweet the sound those
Gm7
C/D
Dm
F/B♭ B♭
B♭/C
Bº E+(♯9)
simple words, "we love you," still echo in my heart; Welcome
Am7
D7(♭9)
G♭M9♯5/D G♭M9♯5/A♭
home, no more will I take this place for granted, it's so
Gm7
F2/A
F/B♭ B♭
Gm7
good to be loved and wanted after you've done wrong,

Medley options: Amazing Grace; Mercy Saw Me.

…How good it is to sing praises to our God… Psalm 147:1 (NIV)

We've Come to Praise Him

969

HM-73

Words and Music by
RICHARD SMALLWOOD

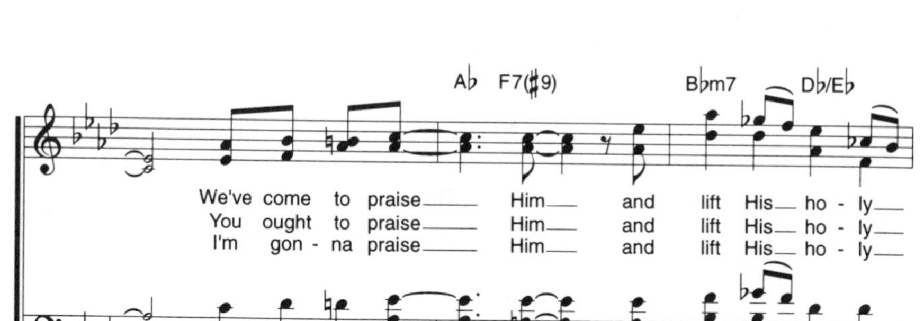

A♭
1,4
A♭/E♭
name.
2. We've come to praise
name.
5. I'm gon - na praise
A♭
2,3.
B♭m
B°
A♭/C
name.
name.
Make a
Make a
VERSE
D♭9
joy - ful noise
un - to the Lord,
joy - ful noise
un - to the Lord,
make a joy - ful noise
make a joy - ful noise

Medley options: Joy in My Heart; God Is Able (ROGERS).

That I may declare your praises in the gates of the Daughter of Zion and there rejoice in your salvation. Psalm 9:14 (NIV)

970 When We All Get to Heaven

HM-70

Words and Music by
ELIZA HEWITT and
EMILY WILSON

Medley options: Put Your Hands Together; One True Living God.

He seized the dragon…who is the devil…and bound him for a thousand years. Revelation 20:2 (NIV)

971 Winna, Mon

HM-74

Words and Music by
LESTER LEWIS

E♭ A♭ E♭ B♭ E♭
1.
Je-sus is the Win-na, Mon, the Win-na, Mon all the time.
E♭ A♭
I am on the win-ning side, the
E♭ B♭
win-ning side, the win-ning side;
E♭ A♭ E♭ B♭ E♭
I am on the win-ning side, the win-ning side all the time.
VERSE 1
Gm
Worship Leader
Cm
In Mat-thew, chap-ter two, Sa-tan lose
3

A♭
B♭
when Je - sus was born in a man - ger;
Gm
Cm
And in the wil - der - ness, Sa - tan lose a - gain,
A♭
de - feat - ed at the Mount of Trans - fig - u - ra -
B♭
All
E♭
B♭
E♭
2.
tion. It is such Win - na, Mon all the time.
VERSE 2
Gm
Worship Leader
Cm
At the cru - ci - fix - ion, Sa - tan lose a - gain,
3

A♭
B♭
3
3
when Je-sus rose tri-um-phant-ly from the grave;
Gm
Cm
3
And at the As-cen-sion, Sa-tan lose
A♭
B♭
once more, when I was born a-gain. It is such
E♭
B♭
E♭
3.
Win-na, Mon all the time. The
A♭/E♭
Win-na, Mon, Win-na, Mon, Win-na, Mon, Win-na, Mon,

Medley option: Righteousness, Peace, Joy.

I will praise you, O Lord my God, with all my heart. Psalm 86:12 (NIV)

With All My Heart

972

HM-72

Words and Music by
MARTIN F. BALL

Em7 D/F♯ Asus A D/F♯
love You, Lord. Let ev - 'ry -
CHORUS
G Em7 G/A A G/A A D F♯m7
thing that is with - in me, bless Your ho - ly
Bm D/A G Em7 G/A A G/A A
name, long - ing and thirst - ing, my spir - it cries to
D C/D D7 G Em7 G/A A G/A A
You; For on - ly in Your pres - ence will
D F♯m7 Bm D/A G2
I be sat - is - fied, You're my de - light, Lord, and

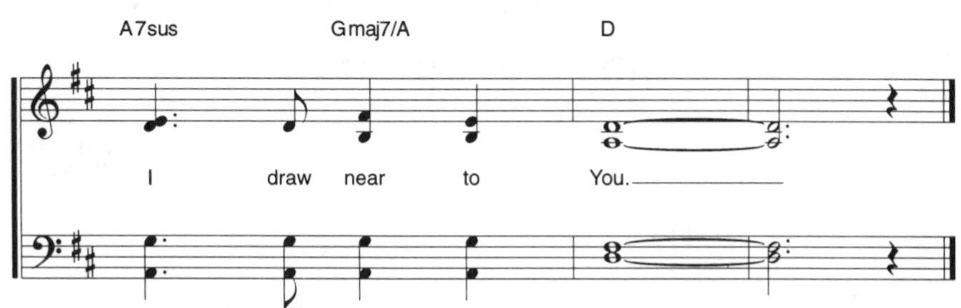

Medley options: I Will Come to You; Change My Heart O God (ESPINOSA).

Love the Lord your God with all your heart…soul…mind and…strength. Mark 12:30 (NIV)

973 With All of Our Heart

HM-69

Words and Music by
DON MOEN and
MARTIN J. NYSTROM

Em7
D/G
A
A/B Bm7
let us de - ter - mine that right at the start we will
we have de - ter - mined that right at the start we will
Em7
G
wor - ship the Fa - ther with all of our
wor - ship You, Je - sus, with all of our
Asus
A
D
Em7
D/F♯
heart. With all of our
heart. With all of our
CHORUS
G
A
D
Em7
D/F♯ G
heart, mind, and strength we give You hon -
A
Bm7
or glo - ry and praise; Not from a - far,

A2/C♯ A/G F♯m7 Bm7
or just with our lips, but all that we are,
Em7 D Gmaj7/A A D Em7 D/F♯
we of - fer in wor - ship. With all of our
G A D Em7 D/F♯ G
heart, mind, and strength, Je - sus, we come
F♯ Bm G D
to lift up Your name; We give You glo -
Em7 D/F♯ G D/A
ry, we give You praise, with all of our heart,

Medley options: Blessed Be the Lord (HAMLIN); I Rejoice in Your Love;
As for Me and My House.

Taste and see that the Lord is good… Psalm 34:8 (NIV)

974

You Are Good

HM-69

Words and Music by
MARTIN J. NYSTROM
and DON HARRIS

F♯m11 G♯7sus G♯7 C♯m
nev - er be the same, I have tast - ed of You, Lord,
C♯m/B Amaj7 F♯m7 A/B
and all that I can say is, "You are
CHORUS
F♯m11 E/G♯ A2 B G♯m7 B/C♯
good!" You are good,
C♯m7 B/C♯ C♯m7 F♯m7 B7sus B7
You are mer - ci - ful to me, and You
G♯m7 C♯m7 C♯m/B F♯m7 E/G♯ A
meet my ev - 'ry need; You are good,

Medley options: For the Lord Is Good; Hallowed Be Thy Name (MASON).

For where two or three come together in my name, there am I with them. Matthew 18:20 (NIV)

You Are Here

975

HM-69

Words and Music by
DON MOEN and
MARTIN J. NYSTROM

E♭ B♭/D Cm A♭2
throned up-on our praise, You are here, here to heal
B♭ E♭ A♭/E♭ E♭ E♭/G
and here to save. You are here
CHORUS
A♭2 E♭/G
in our midst, how we've wait -
Fm7 B♭7sus E♭
ed for mo - ments like this; Have Your way
A♭2 E♭/G
in this place, Ho - ly Spir -

Medley options: As the Deer; He Is Here; In the Presence of Jehovah (DAVIS).

…"Look, the Lamb of God, who takes away the sin of the world!" John 1:29 (NIV)

976 You Are My All in All

HM-71

Words and Music by
DENNIS JERNIGAN

Medley options: Awesome in This Place; We Give You Glory; Unto You.

For great is the Lord and most worthy of praise… 1 Chronicles 16:25 (NIV)

977 You Are Worthy to Be Praised

HM-70

Words and Music by
RICH COOK

Medley options: In the Presence; I Sing Praises.

...Fear not, for I have redeemed you; I have called you by your name; You are Mine. Isaiah 43:1 (NKJ)

978 You Called Me by Name

HM-69

Words and Music by
MARTIN J. NYSTROM
and DON HARRIS

D
me.
ty.
Yet You have
For You have
CHORUS
Bm G2 D G A
called me by name, You are ac - quaint- ed with all of my
Bm G2 D G2 A
ways; Bought by Your blood, drawn by Your love, I am Your
Em11 G Asus A D A/C♯ Bm G2 D
dwell- ing place. For You have called me Your friend, show- ing me
G A Bm G2 D G2
fa - vor, a- gain and a - gain; I'm set a - part, dear to Your

Medley options: He Is Exalted; Come and Behold Him.

I will praise you, O Lord, with all my heart... Psalm 138:1 (NIV)

You're Worthy of My Praise

979

HM-72

Words and Music by
DAVID RUIS

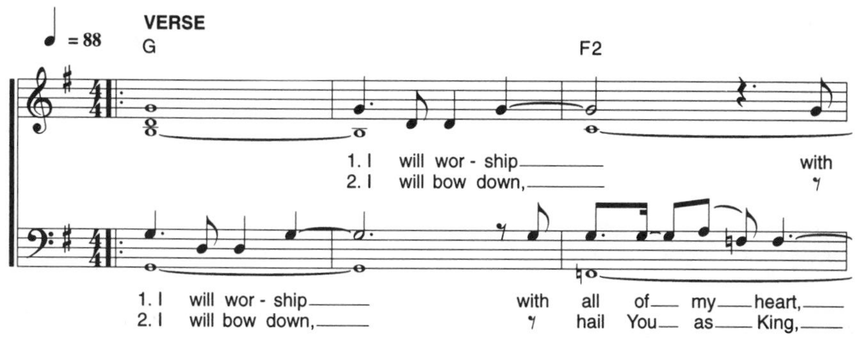

F2
I will seek You
I will lift up
my
all of my days,
my eyes to Your throne,
C
all of my days,
eyes to Your throne,
I will fol - low
I will trust You,
I will fol - low
and I will trust You,
I will
G
Am7
C/D
D
all Your ways.
trust You a -
all of Your ways.
trust You a - lone.
CHORUS
G
D/F♯
C/E
C
I will give You all my wor - ship, I will give You
lone. I will give You all my wor - ship, I will give You

Medley options: Lord, I Lift Your Name on High; We Declare Your Name.

980

You have turned for me my mourning into dancing;
You have put off my sackcloth and clothed me with gladness. Psalm 30:11 (NKJ)

You've Turned My Mourning into Dancing

HM-72

Words and Music by
MARTIN F. BALL, DAVID HADDEN
and KEVIN POTTS

Cm/E♭ Am7(♭5) G/D Em7 Am7
lent, O Lord my God, I will give
C/D G
thanks to You.
VERSE
C F/C C
For You have set me free, brought me new
G D/E E Am7
lib-er-ty, and I can nev-er be the same
C/D D C F/C C
a-gain; I live in vic-to-ry, for Je-sus

G D/E E Am7 C/D
died for me. I want my life to tes -
D Bm7 D/E Em Em7
ti - fy, I want my life to mag - ni - fy; I
C♯m7(♭5) A9 C/D D C/D
2nd time to Coda
want my life to glo - ri - fy Your name.
CHORUS 2
G2 C
How can I hold back, how can I keep si - lent,
Dm/C C G
con - sid - er - ing what God's done for me?

D C/D D G G/F
I was bound by law, by
C/E Cm/E♭ Am7(♭5)
sin and death held cap - tive; But by the
D.S. al Coda
G/D Em7 Am7 C/D G
Spir - it of life I am com - plete - ly free.
Coda
CHORUS 3
G2 C
You've turned my mourn - ing in - to danc -
Dm/C C Dm/C C G
ing, re - moved all my sack -

D C/D D
cloth and clothed me with joy;
G G/F C/E
That my heart may sing to You and not be si-
Cm/E♭ Am7(♭5) G/D Em7 Am7
lent, O Lord my God, I will give
C/D G/D Em7 Am7 C/D
thanks, O Lord, my God, I will give thanks, O Lord,
Bm7 Em7 Am7 C/D
my God, I will give thanks to You.

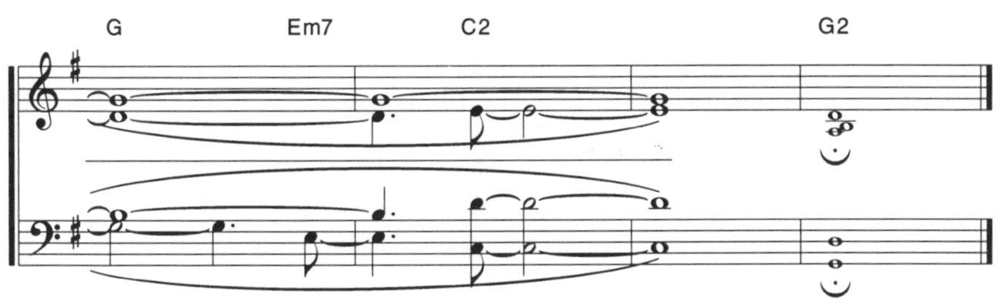

Medley options: O, Clap Your Hands (FUNK); Great Is the Lord (CHRISTENSEN).

INDEX A
INDEX ACCORDING TO KEY AND TEMPO

INDEX B
TOPICAL INDEX

ADORATION

ASSURANCE

BLOOD OF CHRIST

CALL TO WORSHIP

CALL TO WORSHIP, Cont'd

COMMITMENT

CONSECRATION

DECLARATION

DECLARATION, Cont'd

EVANGELISM

GOD THE FATHER

HEALING

HOLY SPIRIT

HYMNS

JESUS, THE SON

JESUS, THE SON, Cont'd

JOY

PRAISE

PRAISE, Cont'd

TESTIMONY

THANKSGIVING

VICTORY

WORD OF GOD

INDEX C
INDEX ACCORDING TO FIRST LINES

INDEX D
INDEX ACCORDING TO SCRIPTURE REFERENCE

INDEX E
INDEX OF COPYRIGHT OWNERS

ALVIN SLAUGHTER MUSIC, c/o Integrity Music, 1000 Cody Rd., Mobile, AL 36695: Selection 903.

BARGAIN BASEMENT MUSIC, (adm. by Integrated Copyright Group) P.O. Box 24149, Nashville, TN 37202: Selection 894.

BUD JOHN SONGS, INC., (adm. by EMI Christian Music Publishing), P.O. Box 5085, 101 Winners Circle, Brentwood, TN 37024-5085: Selection 955.

CENTERGY MUSIC, (adm. by Integrated Copyright Group) P.O. Box 24149, Nashville, TN 37202: Selections 916, 931.

CENTURY OAK PUBLISHING GROUP, (adm. by Copyright Management, Inc.) 1102 17th Avenue South, Suite 400, Nashville, TN 37212: Selections 895, 969.

DARLENE ZSCHECH/HILLSONGS AUSTRALIA, (adm. in U.S. and Canada by Integrity's Hosanna! Music), c/o Integrity Music, Inc., 1000 Cody Rd., Mobile, AL 36695: Selections 926, 947.

DAVISHOP, c/o Integrity Music, Inc., 1000 Cody Rd., Mobile, AL 36695: Selections 902, 960.

EDWARD GRANT CORP., (adm. by BMG Music Publishing), 8370 Wilshire Blvd., Beverly Hills, CA 90211: Selection 893.

EXALTATION MUSIC, (adm. by Ministry Management Associates) P.O. 1248, Decatur, AL 35602-1248: Selection 928.

GAITHER MUSIC COMPANY, adm. by Gaither Copyright Management, P.O. Box 737, Alexandria, IN 46001: Selection 895.

HIGH PRAISES, (adm. by WORD Inc.), 3319 West End Avenue, Suite 200, Nashville, TN 37203: Selection 910.

HIS BANNER PUBLISHING, P.O. Box 142, West Milford, NJ 07480: Selection 934.

HOUSE OF MERCY, (adm. by Maranatha! Music c/o The Copyright Co., Nashville, TN), 40 Music Square East, Nashville, TN 37203: Selection 915.

INTEGRITY'S HOSANNA! MUSIC, c/o Integrity Music, 1000 Cody Rd., Mobile, AL 36695: Selections 886, 890, 891, 894, 896, 898, 899, 901, 902, 903, 904, 905, 906, 907, 908, 909, 911, 913, 914, 916, 917, 918, 919, 921, 927, 929, 930, 931, 933, 936, 937, 941, 942, 943, 944, 945, 946, 948, 950, 952, 953, 954, 959, 960, 961, 963, 965, 966, 968, 970, 971, 972, 973, 974, 975, 978, 980.

INTEGRITY'S PRAISE! MUSIC, c/o Integrity Music, Inc., 1000 Cody Rd., Mobile, AL 36695: Selections 897, 932, 938, 956.

JOHN EZZY, DANIEL GRUL, STEPHAN McPHERSON/HILLSONGS AUSTRALIA, (adm. in U.S. and Canada by Integrity's Hosanna! Music), c/o Integrity Music Inc., 1000 Cody Rd., Mobile, AL 36695: Selection 925

JUNIPER LANDING MUSIC, (adm. by Word Music), 3319 West End Avenue, Suite 200, Nashville, TN 37203: Selection 932.

KINGSWAY'S THANKYOU MUSIC, (adm. in the Northern Hemisphere by EMI Christian Music Publishing, P.O. Box 5085, 101 Winners Circle, Brentwood, TN 37024-5085: Selection 887, 964.

KIRK HENDERSON PUBLISHING, 1413 Woodfield Drive, Nashville, TN 37211: Selection 897.

MANNA MUSIC, 35255 Brooten Road, Pacific City, OR 97135: Selection 889.

MARANATHA! MUSIC, c/o The Copyright Company, 40 Music Square East, Nashville, TN 37203: Selection 892, 979.

MERCY PUBLISHING, c/o Music Services, 209 Chapelwood Drive, Franklin, TN 37064: Selection 958.

MERCY/VINEYARD PUBLISHING, c/o Music Services, 209 Chapelwood Drive, Franklin, TN 37064: Selections 935, 951, 967.

NEW SPRING PUBLISHING, (a div. of Brentwood-Benson Music Publishing Inc.), 741 Cool Springs Blvd., Franklin, TN 37067: Selection 922.

RESTORATION MUSIC LTD, (adm. worldwide except Europe by Integrity's Hosanna! Music, adm. in Europe by Sovereign Music UK) c/o Integrity Music, Inc., 1000 Cody Rd., Mobile, AL 36695: Selections 904, 919, 927, 963, 980.

RCM ENTERPRISES, 3402 West MacArthur Blvd., Suite F, Santa Anna, CA 92704: Selection 977.

RICHWOOD MUSIC, (adm. by Copyright Management, Inc.) 1102 17th Avenue South, Suite 400, Nashville, TN 37212: Selections 895, 969.

RIVER OAKS MUSIC COMPANY, (adm. by EMI Christian Music Publishing), P.O. Box 5085, 101 Winners Circle, Brentwood, TN 37024-5085: Selection 924.

ROBERT EASTWOOD/HILLSONGS AUSTRALIA, (adm. in U.S. and Canada by Integrity's Hosanna! Music), c/o Integrity Music, Inc., 1000 Cody Rd., Mobile, AL 36695: Selection 900.

RUSSELL FRAGAR/HILLSONGS AUSTRALIA, (adm. in U.S. and Canada by Integrity's Hosanna! Music), c/o Integrity Music, Inc., 1000 Cody Rd., Mobile, AL 36695: Selections 888, 912, 939, 949.

SCRIPTURE IN SONG, (a div. of Integrity Music, Inc.) 1000 Cody Rd., Mobile, AL 36695: Selection 957.

SHADE TREE PUBLISHING, c/o The Copyright Co., 40 Music Square East, Nashville, TN 37203: Selection 979.

SHEPHERD'S HEART MUSIC, INC., (adm. by WORD, Inc.), c/o Word, Inc., 3319 West End Avenue, Suite 200, Nashville, TN 37203: Selection 976.

WORD MUSIC, (a div. of WORD, Inc.) c/o Word, Inc., 3319 West End Avenue, Suite 200, Nashville, TN 37203: Selections 920, 923, 940, 962.

YELLOW HOUSE MUSIC, (adm. by Brentwood-Benson Music Publishing Inc.), 741 Cool Springs Blvd., Franklin, TN 37067: Selection 924.